Collaborate or Die

HOW BEING A JERK KILLS IDEAS AND CAREERS

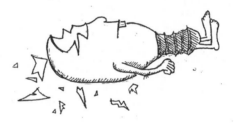

BRETT CRAIG

ISBN-13: 978-0692417201
ISBN-10: 0692417206

Cover design by Adam Hale
Editing by Zoe Markham
Book illustrations © 2016 Brett Craig
Author photograph by Neph Trejo

DEDICATION

To my teachers, Mary Ruth Curlee and Mark Secrist, who first planted the idea of a career in advertising long ago. To Gary Schaffer for opening the door to a career. To my mother, Janice, who taught me the power of humility. Special thanks to Breezy, my wife, who is my sounding board, my best friend and most trusted advisor. Finally, to my Lord, Jesus Christ, who's counter-intuitive truth inspires the ideas that fill these pages.

FOREWORD

I remember the first time I met Brett. Deutsch LA was pitching us (Taco Bell) creative ideas for the Super Bowl. The ideas they presented were great. The only problem was Super Bowl 47 was less than two months away.

Less than two months to bring an entire Super Bowl marketing program to life?

Insane.

We knew it was going to be a very challenging assignment and having never worked with Brett or Deutsch LA, we were anxious. Absurd deadlines, a new agency and a Super Bowl effort on the line, demanded that we all – client and agency - check our egos. From the beginning, there was an uncomfortable amount of give and take on both sides. This was a brand new relationship, after all, and this was the Super Bowl, the grandest of all marketing stages. Yet despite this, as we continued to work with Brett and Deutsch LA, we formed an uncommon collaborative bond. Consequently, you could feel the Super Bowl idea take on a life of it's own and get even better as we opened our minds, respectfully debated ideas and operated as a true team.

After a highly successful Super Bowl effort, the collaboration continued. The trust between Taco Bell and Deutsch LA grew too. And with this trust, we continued to push the bounds of the work for Taco Bell. Our next big assignment was the launch of Taco Bell's breakfast menu. As a late-night brand attempting to break into a morning game dominated by McDonalds, we needed to create as much disruption and conversation as possible with our advertising.

Deutsch LA presented a brash idea in which real people named "Ronald McDonald" would express their love for Taco Bell's new breakfast. It was a concept so inherently controversial, so scary, our partnership with Deutsch would be tested all over again. Luckily, the trust and collaborative spirit we had developed was so strong, that a year later (after watching the idea die and come back to life multiple times) one of the most famous pieces of work in Taco Bell's history was finally born.

But beyond my experiences working at Taco Bell, over the past 15 years I have had the pleasure of working on some truly amazing campaigns, award winning campaigns - both agency and client side. As I look back now, collaboration has been the cornerstone of every truly great piece of work – it's that simple.

So how do you collaborate successfully?

That's what this book is all about.

What I appreciated most is that Brett uses real-life case studies that demonstrate what great collaboration really looks like. And what you discover through these stories is that collaboration is an intentional choice. It takes effort. But the payoff can be huge.

I choose to collaborate. Read this book and I'm betting you will too.

Aron North
Director of Advertising & Branded Content, Taco Bell

CONTENTS

PREFACE

While there is a virtual sea of business books on "Leadership", the subject of Collaboration is one that seems to be woefully underestimated in terms of its importance. I believe, natural talent aside, the question of whether a person can effectively collaborate with others is the single most important factor in determining whether that person's ideas will consistently see the light of day.

Every day we see the ill effects of people who do not collaborate effectively: in professional sports, in the political arena, and most certainly in business, where organizations can be massively crippled by poor collaboration.

In my particular industry of Advertising, for example, we are increasingly required to work with multiple agency partners in the service of a single brand, a model that's being adopted industry-wide. It can be hard to work well with people within the walls of your own building, let alone with outside entities with competing interests and ideas.

While I believe collaboration is challenging for everyone, my main focus in this book is that it's *especially* challenging for creative people. This is because creative people are cut from a slightly different cloth – sometimes a bit offbeat, often a little rebellious, and almost always accustomed to following their own artistic voice. Strong, individualistic personalities make the world of creativity interesting and dynamic; yet often, these same traits can make collaborating well with others a daunting challenge for creative people, even, at times, impossible.

Adding to the challenge, we of the creative stripe tend to be both self-centered and insecure at the same time. We want "credit" for our ideas, since ownership of them is the key to advancement in our career; yet this desire for "credit" can stand in the way of improving our ideas, because when we circle the wagons around our concepts - in order to keep control and ownership of them - we lose the opportunity to make them *better*.

My goal here is not to explore "why" creative people struggle with collaboration – I'm going to make the assumption that, if you're reading this, you already know it's true. The goal of this book is to give creative people a practical – and applicable – overview of what it takes to effectively collaborate with others in the pursuit of creating brilliant ideas.

This book will not offer you a dry academic theory on what makes for great collaboration; but observations born of hands-on experience. In fact, I repeatedly use real-world examples, citing stories from my career in advertising, working for some of the most well-known agencies and brands in the world.

However, this is not in itself a book about advertising, nor is it a book just for advertising mad men and women. This book is for anyone who must collaborate in the pursuit of bringing great ideas to life. That's virtually every creative person in the world, including designers, inventors, advertising writers and art directors, architects, filmmakers, animators, software and game developers – just about anyone whose job requires that they work well with others in the pursuit of creating brilliant ideas.

This book was also written with students, and people who have only recently entered the work force, in mind. The fact is, it's likely that no one will ever teach you how to collaborate well. Certainly no one ever spoke to me about this subject. Oh, you may see the odd corporate poster on the wall, with a canoe full of people rowing the same direction and a caption that says something like, "Teamwork". And, yes, everyone instinctively knows from preschool on that you're supposed to "play nice" with others.

Yet more often than not, when you enter the workforce, you'll see something quite different: jealousy, backbiting and ego often undermining any attempt at real collaboration.

For some creative people, a book about "collaboration" in the pursuit of producing exceptional ideas may seem unpalatable. After all, we tend to celebrate visionary individuals when we celebrate great acts of creativity – be they products, theories, inventions, movies or more.

Well, knock yourself out trying to be the next da Vinci, Edison or Steve Jobs. There are only a handful of these people in every generation. Personally, I'd rather remain somewhat anonymous, but have a long and successful career, doing what I love, being a part of many creative projects and seeing them come to life. This is what having a collaborative spirit has allowed me to do to this very day.

It's my hope, on reading this book, you'll see that being a great collaborator can do exactly the same for you.

Brett Craig
January 2016

1

CAN'T COLLABORATE? BECOME A SCULPTOR

Someone in advertising once said to me that, if you want to create ideas on your own, with no input or influence from anyone else, you should become a sculptor. I don't know any sculptors, but I imagine that while they enjoy total control of their creations, I'm not sure many of them are able to make a living at it. Even worse, since many creative people like the world to see and appreciate what they make, there's a danger of it being a frustrating career path in more ways than one.

In any case, the implication of the become-a-sculptor example is obvious: advertising, like most creative fields, is about generating brilliant ideas through collaboration; if you can't collaborate, then you can't really create anything in advertising.

You may be thinking, "But what about people like Steve Jobs? Didn't he steamroll people in the pursuit of creating world-changing products? Aren't the best creative ideas the product of a singular, brilliant vision of a single person?"

First of all, you're no Steve Jobs. Don't take it personally, I'm certainly no Jobs either. In fact, 99.9% of us are not in the intellectual league of the preeminent creative visionaries of our generation. As I mentioned in the preface, there are only so many da Vincis, Michelangelos, Edisons and, yes, Steve Jobs in the world.

Since we've established that neither of us is Steve Jobs, let's think about him a little more. Jobs was a creative personality known for his brilliance, but equally for his impatience, stubbornness and single-minded vision that often alienated a good portion of the people around him. The truth is, those very qualities we collectively admired him for also - at least in part - got him forced out of the company he started. That's hard to believe: to be fired from the board of the company you founded in your own garage. Steve Jobs lost 12 years helming the company he loved. Understand, I'm not suggesting that Jobs was anything but a massive success. I'm also not suggesting that people don't learn things from the setbacks, twists and turns their careers inevitably take – Jobs himself said he learned a lot from his time away from Apple. However, I *am* suggesting that Jobs lost the reigns – for years - of one of the most innovative companies in modern history, in part, because he was extremely hard to collaborate with.

But the real point I'm making here is this: if one of the most brilliant CEOs and creative minds in modern history could be fired from the company he created, what happens to mere mortals of more modest creative abilities – like you and me - when we chose not to, or are unable to, effectively collaborate?

You get the point: to create great ideas, products, digital ideas, start-ups – anything creative at all, really - you must be able to collaborate well with people. To achieve success in any creative project, to make a living in any creative field, you must be able to work with others in such a way that you can produce excellent outcomes, consistently. If not, you'll eventually find yourself out of a job and sculpting in a garage, where the only people who will ever appreciate what you make will likely be your mom, and some close friends who'll tell you your sculptures are wonderful (although, strangely, they'll never seem to want to buy one).

2

COLLABORATION IS INEVITABLE ANYWAY

Few things will better reveal how well you collaborate in the pursuit of brilliant ideas than working in an advertising agency. There may be fields that demand more collaboration and cooperation, but if there are, it's doubtful those fields have as many egotists, narcissists and megalomaniacs as you'll find in advertising. They don't call us Mad Men for nothing.

And yet, collaborate we must. It's inescapable. And we must do it well or our product (ideas) will suffer and our clients will surely fire us (some of those megalomaniacs reside on the client side, just for the record, and their itchy fingers are never far from the "fire" button.)

As an Executive Creative Director who's worked with a great amount of high-profile brands like Pepsi, Dr Pepper, Taco Bell and PlayStation, I've learned a lot about collaboration, including just how hard it is to do well. As an Executive Creative Director, who's job it is to shape and execute ideas, you're at the center of a wheel with many spokes, and you've got to have them all working together to keep the wheels from falling off the idea. To illustrate my point, let's look at what it takes to make the modern day thirty-second commercial, the ubiquitous advertising commercial unit that has appeared on TV for the last 40 years.

First, it takes two creative people - a copywriter and an art director - who must work together to create an idea worth shooting. (This in and of itself is worthy of a book on cooperation since copywriter and art director teams spend more time with each other than their spouses; but I digress). This idea, once generated, will need to be seen and approved by any number of internal agency people, depending on the nature of the commercial. For this example, let's say it's a Super Bowl commercial. No less than 10-20 different people will touch it within the agency – either by offering an opinion, having to give their approval or directly affecting the actual idea in a profound way.

From here, the commercial will need to go to clients for approval - lots of clients. Clients have all kinds of opinions. Some opinions are smart and some are just plain scary. Junior clients, mid-level clients and senior clients will affect it, and then the really senior clients above the senior clients will affect it some more. Then, since it's the Super Bowl and the client is spending at least 3.5 million bucks on the media slot alone, the board of directors may want to comment on it and offer some suggestions. So will the CEO, of course, and, I'm not kidding you, so might his or her son or daughter. It happens, believe me.

I would venture to say that this commercial will have been reviewed, commented on and touched by no less than 30-50 people by now, including potentially the CEO's daughter.

But we're not done.

The commercial – amazingly - is still alive, even after the CEO's daughter convinced her daddy that Miley Cyrus would be a bigger hit in the Super Bowl than Jay Z, thus potentially killing your career forever because you'll have used Miley Cyrus (no offense, Miley) in your commercial. But luckily, Miley is not available because she recently pulled a hamstring while twerking, so she'll have to pass. Thank goodness. Hello, Jay Z. (The above is in no way based on a true situation, but these are the kind of things that happen in advertising all the time.)

So your commercial is still alive, and more or less intact now that you're over the Miley hurdle. But now you've got to bring this idea to life in the form of a film. And since your last name isn't Spielberg, you're going to need to hire a director. Did I mention something earlier about megalomaniacs and narcissists? A Director, especially a high-profile one, is quite accustomed to asserting – and doggedly sticking to - his or her vision. In my experience, some – ok, many - don't seem to be altruistic collaborators, like you and I. And strangely, though you came up with the idea to begin with and you only hired them a day ago, they act more like it's their idea than yours. Point is, you just signed up for a crash-course in collaboration.

The director has a massive crew that will be doing everything from building sets, to controlling the lighting and look of your film, to making sure you have a decent place to sit and watch the action as the director directs your idea as if he or she came up with it.

Dozens of people on the set are now touching your idea, affecting your idea, shaping your idea, along with you. And when you're done, you'll have to work with an editor, a colorist, and special effects houses in order to make sure it comes out as brilliantly as you first hoped it might.

By now you may want to become a sculptor after all – all this collaboration could kill you and your idea. But let's face it, this is the reality of creating a commercial, and this is the reality of creating *almost anything creative* today.

How many people are involved in making an iPad – from conceiving it, designing it and actually making it? How many people are involved in making a state-of-the-art high-rise from a blueprint to actually constructing it? What about making a movie? How about a mobile app? A website? A new social-media platform?

Are you starting to get the picture? Collaboration is inevitable, essential, and, as you'll see, often very beneficial. You must do it well as a creative person so you can see your ideas come to life.

Or…

…You must become a sculptor.

3

DON'T BE SO PARANOID

Something strange happens when creative people have ideas: they get paranoid about them. They're afraid someone is going to maim them, or kill them. They fear someone else is going to try to take credit for them, that people won't know that they were the genius that came up with the idea. They worry that some small-minded person won't understand the idea. They worry that someone else might have the same idea. They worry that someone might steal their idea.

This, by the way, is all before they've even written the idea down.

And this paranoia only grows throughout the process of bringing the idea to life, as all of these fears come into play over and over again.

So what do creative people do? They build a wall around their idea. They try to protect it by avoiding input. When they're forced to share it, they get defensive instead of really listening to see if there's anything additive in what someone else might be saying about their idea.

This reaction in creative people is understandable. It's just a by-product of human nature: wanting to protect something perceived as hard-earned and valuable. But these fears, this paranoia that every creative person feels to one degree or another, will stop you from consistently creating great work, because it will make you incapable of collaborating with others in a brilliant and productive way.

Why?

Because when you get paranoid about sharing your idea, your idea often never gets any better, or, even worse, it never gets made a reality at all.

You need to believe that your idea can always be better, and understand that the key to making it better is sharing it with other smart, collaborative people.

You have to believe this. You have to internalize this. If you don't, you will not consistently achieve anything of consequence, creatively speaking. Eventually, you'll find yourself out of the creative career you love and in a garage, sculpting.

But again, in order to share your idea, you'll have to open yourself up to what others *think* of your idea. You'll have to let other people criticize, question and embellish said idea. You'll need to occasionally let people say silly things about it, things that sometimes may appear to make no sense the first time you hear them, or never end up making sense at all. People talking about your idea may feel akin to someone talking about your child, but trust me, this process is really healthy for your idea.

Here's why: the best ideas are usually just glimpses of something at first - a flash of inspiration, an intuition, a word, an image, a sentence maybe. At least that's how it's always been for me. Sometimes, in these moments, I might glimpse a lot of the potential idea and it all begins to pour out. Other times, it's just a limited glimpse, but your gut says there's something big there. Either way, by sharing these first intuitive thoughts/notions/ideas with other smart, collaborative people, these thoughts begin to grow flesh, maybe a pair of legs and then one day they walk upright, right out of your mind, and into the world. That's how it has worked for me my entire career.

When this process is going well, it's like a great jam session: people – with different talents and perspectives – begin to add to this tapestry, this song of an idea. And it's amazing how fast things start to take shape as you're brainstorming, adding to and subtracting from your idea with other people who want to make the idea better. It's like tripling or quadrupling your brainpower and your creativity, and your idea can often take exponential leaps. But to do this you can't get all paranoid about sharing. And you can't be threatened by letting people play with your idea. I'm not suggesting you cast your pearl of an idea before swine – be judicious about who you do this with, by all means – but share your idea you must if you want to create truly *great* ideas and products.

I am not terribly threatened by what people think of my ideas (okay, maybe I'm a little scared of what my wife thinks of them. When she doesn't like things, she's usually right.) In fact, I actually seek out opinions and don't care where they're coming from either, for the most part. Of course, I value some opinions more than others. But I find it's an opportunity to get a real, unbiased reaction and uncover some kernel of truth about the idea. Sometimes, I expose an idea to different people and hear the same comment about it from multiple sources – surely that's input worth considering. Sometimes, I hear a fatal flaw in the idea that I didn't consider. And, every once in awhile, I hear that dreaded phrase, "that's been done before by such and such".

Yet even when I hear unpleasant things about my idea, at least I know what its weaknesses might be. I know what I need to do to it for it to be stronger or, in some cases, for it to be a viable idea again. Occasionally, as I'm talking to different people about the idea, I realize I should cut bait, move on to a new idea because of an unfixable flaw. Other times, if I'm really listening for the truth about the idea, a piece of input I receive will be added to it, and this additional thought, this flourish, often takes the idea to a whole new level.

Of course, I will defend aspects of ideas that I believe are worth defending and oppose embellishments that are not worthy additions. But I'm never afraid to let people turn my idea over and see if there are any cracks in the veneer, or, maybe add a new detail to it. And then, wake up the next day and change something about it again, if my team and I think it makes it better.

Why?

Because I've often discovered I like the idea even more after exposing it to other people's input and opinions. And if I don't like what the idea has become after doing so, well, often I can just change it back. Ideas are malleable creatures, in the end.

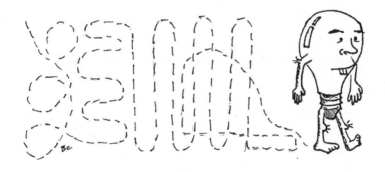

This is the inevitable journey of an idea. Forwards. Backwards. Sideways. Addition. Subtraction. Addition, again. And sometimes, even, returning to the beginning when you realize you've lost an essential element somewhere along the way. Ideas are rarely, if ever, fully whole at birth. They gestate. They evolve. They grow arms and legs. And the process that accelerates this journey and makes an idea whole begins when you expose the idea to other intelligent, collaborative people.

You'll never know your idea's true potential, you'll never experience exponential leaps in your idea, if you don't share it and allow others to collaborate with you in the pursuit of making it better. And sharing it is not enough, you have to share it with a genuine desire to listen and understand people's input.

This is how ideas become brilliant, faster. If you're paranoid about sharing your idea, you won't be able to do this. Even if you're forced by the process to share your idea, you won't be able to see the validity in the feedback, since you're too paranoid to really listen. Not only will your idea suffer, in the end, so will your career.

So, make an effort to reject paranoia and open your mind to people's input, feedback and embellishments. I promise you, at the very least, you will learn valuable things about your idea that make it better, stronger and more viable. And you'll also be the kind of person people love collaborating with, which means you'll be making more brilliant ideas in the future.

4

IT'S ABOUT THE IDEA, NOT YOU

From left: That's me (star struck) and advertising Hall-of-Famer, Lee Clow.

One of the greatest creative minds I had the good fortune to watch and learn from, was Lee Clow. Lee is perhaps the most famous creative in the history of advertising, responsible for some of the most iconic work ever done, including what is considered the greatest commercial in history (the commercial all Super Bowl commercials have since tried to emulate in terms of fame, "1984"), directed by

Ridley Scott.

Lee Clow also happened to be my boss at TBWA/Chiat/Day, Los Angeles. I worked directly with him on various projects over a period of 12 years. If there's one thing I learned watching and working with Lee, it's this: Lee did not care about anything but the idea. He did not care about your ego. He did not care if you were his niece. He did not care if you were the CEO, the art director he loved, the writer he disliked, the client who paid the bills or the account person charged with making the client happy. Lee only cared about ideas and he was only interested in any person or any idea that helped make the creative product better. That's it. End of story. Period.

I love telling stories about Lee. Once, my partner and I had an idea for Sony PlayStation that I thought was great. So did my immediate boss, who brought Lee up to see it. Without so much as a "Hi", Lee began to look over the work pinned on the wall. And without flinching, he began to tear down ideas he disliked, while leaving up ideas he liked. I was watching many ideas – ideas I liked and were *mine* – being thrown into the trash without so much as a conversation.

Watching this I said to Lee, somewhat tongue-in-cheek, "You're hurting our feelings, Lee". He stopped, looked over his shoulder at me and said without an ounce of remorse, "We don't care about that".

Far from being wounded, I laughed at his answer and was, frankly, inspired. There was nothing personal in Lee's evaluation of the work and that in itself was incredibly refreshing. He didn't care about my feelings, he cared about the work, the ideas. In one quick interaction with Lee, I understood that the person at the head of my agency – an agency in the business of creating ideas – truly only cared about those ideas.

My interaction with Lee could have gone badly. If it had been about me and not the idea, I would have taken his feedback the wrong way. If it had been about me and not the idea, I would have thought Lee was a jerk. If it had been about me and not the idea, I would have gone home licking my wounds, and I might have concluded that I ought to take up another career, like, say, sculpting.

If it had been about me and not the idea, I couldn't have collaborated with Lee, really accepted his feedback and then used that input to sharpen and cull the work.

With Lee, you learned early-on it was about the idea, not your feelings or your ego. This was a fairly easy concept for me to accept. Maybe it was because the lesson was coming from a grey-bearded man, who possessed super-creative powers and looked like Gandalf from *The Lord of the Rings*. Perhaps it's because I don't esteem my own ideas too highly, I don't know; yet this ability to look past my own nose to recognize it isn't about me, it's about the idea, is something I credit as a key reason for my own success.

However, the longer I'm in the advertising business, the more creative people I encounter who cannot grasp this concept. For them, ideas are extensions of their own egos and self-esteem. In fact, ideas are not just ideas, they are actually little versions of themselves. To change their idea is to assault their very person. Like a mother who can't bear the thought that her little junior is the terror of the preschool class, they are not open to be instructed or advised on how to make their brat-of-an-idea better. Even well-meaning, talented people (with far more sensitivity than my former boss, Lee Clow) cannot help these people. And since they cannot help these people, can't collaborate with these people, these people's ideas most often stay a little brat and never grow up to become anything special in the world.

When you understand that it's about the idea, not you, you and your idea are able to achieve amazing things. You are able to hear the wisdom in the suggestions of your boss, co-worker, partner or friend.

You expand your understanding of your own idea by really hearing how others perceive it (after all, most ideas will ultimately need to be appreciated by many others unless you want to be a sculptor). You are able to avoid pitfalls to the idea that you might've overlooked. Also, people will want you and your ideas to succeed, because they see you aren't about politics or ego, you're about ideas. People REALLY like that. People want to be a part of that. People see that their contributions will be appreciated and utilized - which makes your idea better and, yes, *you* a success.

When you know it's all about the idea and not you, you are able to collaborate better. It's as simple as that. And through collaboration your idea has the chance to become better than it is. Who doesn't want that?

5

NON-COLLABORATIVE PEOPLE STINK

Sooner or later – probably sooner – you're going to run into one: a non-collaborative person. (Non-collaborative person, from this point forward will be written as "NP", so I can avoid developing Carpal Tunnel Syndrome.) You may be working with one of these malcontented, self-anointed geniuses right now.

NPs are threatened by everyone around them. They are threatened by every new idea. They do not believe anyone can make them or their idea better. They are insecure in the extreme, but they are also exhibit the flip side of that emotional coin: they're incredibly conceited and cocksure that they – and they alone – possess the knowledge to make the idea great.

Make no mistake, NPs are most assuredly out for themselves.

NPs are visibly annoyed anytime anyone offers even the smallest suggestion because it's not about the idea, it's about them. Their ego is on the line anytime you're talking about the idea. These people are not open to debate; they do not want to turn the idea over, see if it can be optimized or strengthened in some way. NPs are too paranoid and insecure to share their thinking, choosing instead to believe their idea was fully mature when it came out of the womb – that there's no need to grow it up, comb its hair or think about how it will be dressed before it greets the world.

Perhaps the most exhausting part of dealing with NPs is this: they believe they are more noble human beings than you and I. After all, they reason, they simply have the guts to stand up for great concepts and the courage to defend the undefiled purity of their ideas.

We compromise, the NP champions.

We lack conviction, the NP is cocksure.

We are small thinkers, the NP is a big thinker.

The truth is, the NP is a self-centered jerk who drains the energy of every single person around them. The irony is that they themselves are often the biggest obstacle to the potential success of their own idea.

But you know who suffers most? (Ok, next to the poor people

who have to work with these narcissists?) The NP. The NP may succeed in navigating his idea through the system once or twice – batting down every suggestion along the way. But also along the way he made enemies, or, at the very least, found himself with no supporters. The NP makes it to the very end of the process – his idea undefiled (so he thinks) – only to find no one has taken the ride with him. His only hope now? That his idea is a massive success and he can do a solo victory lap. Of course, there will be no one cheering for him, since the NP is a go-it-alone type.

Yet somewhere along the way, on another project, his idea will fail, since all creative people birth ideas that fail eventually. And when his idea fails, people won't care and may even quietly applaud. He may then find himself out of a job, and when this happens, he picks up his iPhone only to find that no one is answering his calls. Suddenly, there are no leads, no messages in his LinkedIn inbox.

See, people hate working with NPs. They don't play nice. They don't share credit. They're an energy-suck.

I've worked in advertising for nearly 20 years and what I just described is not opinion, it's fact. I have had an NP for a partner, an NP for a director, NPs on the client-side, I've dealt with NP celebrities and on and on. With few exceptions, every person of this nature is gone, put out to pasture or struggling on the fringes of their respective occupations. They hop from place to place believing everyone around them is to blame.

But they are to blame. They couldn't collaborate.

So what do you do when you find yourself working alongside an NP?

You're inevitably going to have to deal with an NP when you're trying to collaborate with others, so what do you do when you find yourself in close working proximity to one of these people? Run. I'm half-kidding, but the point is, sometimes it is best to move on; but sometimes moving on is just not possible. So, you're going to have to do something really unpleasant: confront the NP.

As I said, whenever possible, my first reaction is to stay far away from NPs and their self-created, soul-sucking misery. They will do their best to take you and the idea down with their antics. When I see a client who's an NP, I try and avoid them. I've quite literally left a job to remove myself from the influence of an NP client. You can't win with these types – they are not interested in a collaborative, respectful relationship, making it impossible for you to do anything good for them.

In reality, distancing yourself from NPs is not always possible (or even the most mature way to handle the situation). Usually you have to try and make it work, at least for a period of time – till the project is over. But then what?

In my experience, if it's someone you must collaborate with on a daily basis, you've got to nicely, but confidently, confront him or her. You simply work too closely, and with too much at stake, to tolerate NP behavior. They've got to see that that kind of behavior is counter-productive and miserable for you to be around. You may need to have multiple people point this out to the NP – a quasi-intervention, if you will – since NPs rarely admit they are this way. I've found NPs act surprised when you confront their behavior, but confront them you must.

By confronting the behavior you set boundaries, letting the NP know that's not how you want to work. By confronting them you show you are a collaborator, yes, but you are no pushover. By confronting them you make it possible to repair the situation – in the best case, forever. In the worst case, maybe just enough to get through the project because at least the person has been made aware of how their behavior is affecting others.

More than likely, if you approach the discussion right, there should be some improvement. I've often found these folks don't even realize how unbearable they are (or they at least feign that they don't know). Either way, you owe the person the truth as you see it. Often, you'll discover there are things you're contributing to the situation as well. Sometimes, it just takes a small adjustment on your part to find the NP suddenly has a new attitude.

On the other hand, if you don't diplomatically, but confidently, confront the NP, I promise they're not going to wake up one morning and decide to change their attitude. It will get worse. Way, way, worse. If you're like most people, you'll find yourself massively distracted by this person's behavior, affecting your productivity and, ultimately, your ideas.

In my experience the worst of the NPs are really just bullies – albeit emotional bullies. What I've found every single time, in my own career, is that confrontation by a confident collaborative-type is the equivalent of a punch in the teeth: the NP shatters EVERY SINGLE TIME. Perhaps it's because on some level they know they're intolerable, selfish, emotionally bullying and totally non-collaborative. By confronting them, you unmask them for the insecure person they know themselves to be. (By the way, you won't be the first person who's ever told them they are this way – of course, deep down they know they are this way – they've likely been behaving this way their whole life.)

If confronting the NP is not feasible (say it's a powerful client), does not work – give it a couple of shots before you give up – or if your work environment fosters rivalries and self-centered behavior, then see my first piece of advice:

Move on.

Life is too short. As a creative person, we all have finite windows of brilliance and productivity – some longer, some shorter – but the window closes eventually. Why waste those precious productive minutes working with an NP, or in an environment that tolerates this behavior?

Looking back, in many situations, I wish I would have confronted (or moved on) much sooner, because the moment I was around collaborative people again, my ideas and I would flourish immediately. While it won't be easy, you'll be doing the right thing by confronting the situation/person. And if it doesn't work? Move on and get back to collaborating with people that make you and your ideas, better.

In the end, non-collaborative people, sadly and inevitably, find themselves alone.

There's simply no one left willing to collaborate with them.

6

TRUST THE PROCESS

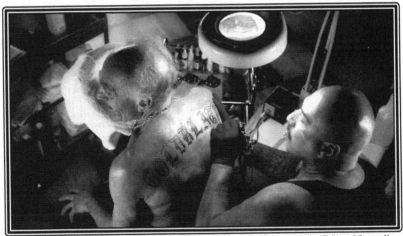

Above: A scene from Taco Bell's 2013 Super Bowl Commercial, "Viva Young".

In my almost 20 years in advertising as a creative, I've created some real duds – that's the nature of creativity, so I just accept that going in. I've also created some things I'm very proud of – pieces of advertising that seem to rise above simply being an "ad" to something that is semi-reminiscent of art (okay, I'm not talking Michelangelo here, I'm just saying they're a little better than your typical ad-schlock). On the whole, I've managed to consistently make work that I'm proud of over the years. And I've managed to do it collaborating with various bosses, partners, directors, editors, digital specialists, brands and clients.

One thing I've learned, and this is absolutely critical for good collaboration, is that you must: *Trust the Process*

What exactly does trusting the process mean? For me, it's simply this: the right ideas, the right outcomes generally emerge through the natural rigor of the creative process that's in place.

If you're surrounded with subpar talent you can probably throw all this out the door – and some people reading might already be thinking, "Well, that's my situation". Not so fast, buddy, are you sure you aren't actually an NP? The truth is, if the group, small business or company you're a part of is successful at all it means there are some folks with a modicum of talent around you. So let's just assume some decently talented folks surround you. Well then, you've got to *trust the process.*

What that means is, you've got to trust in the people around you, that they can get their part of the job done, that they, in fact, possess skills you do not and that they have the power to make the idea better. It means you must trust that ultimately people will collectively arrive at the right conclusions/decisions most of the time. Notice I did not say "all the time", but most of the time. We do not live in a perfect world and the "process" is never perfect, but in the overall process I have faith – and have been proven right most times in my own career – that the right outcomes will ultimately be produced.

Trusting the process is a hard thing to do for most people, even the most collaborative people. Your mind is constantly assessing all the things that can go wrong in the process – all the people that could ruin your idea. And you're sure that only stubborn, willful people who pound their fists on tables get stuff through multilayered, political organizations such as yours. I'm here to tell you the above is not true. I'll say it again: It's not true.

Working on a Super Bowl commercial for Taco Bell in 2013, the stakes were high. The Super Bowl is the most-watched event in the United States with roughly 40% of all households tuning in for the big game. A 60-second media slot costs 7-8 million dollars and over 100 million people will view it live. The commercial will have a pre-life and after-life on the web, which in the case of one Super Bowl commercial by Deutsch LA called "Mini Darth", it received 60 million more views online. Yes, 60 million clicks online – that's because the Super Bowl may be the one event in which people look forward to, and actually want to see, the commercials.

To say the pressure is on in this environment is an understatement. To say people feel some angst during the Super Bowl regarding their commercial – both in the agency and on the client side – is an even bigger understatement. And rightfully so, they have just spent upwards of 10 million dollars teasing, promoting and creating their commercial.

The CEO is watching. Their board of directors will be watching. The shareholders are watching. The whole country is watching. Yeah, there's some serious angst about Super Bowl commercials.

For brands, and the agencies that serve them, there is no bigger stage and consequently no bigger opportunity for overthink, fear, hand-wringing, second-guessing and for collaboration to break down for fear of failure – for fear of the process not working out and the idea failing on the grandest of stages for all to see.

This was one very important project. For starters, there was the agency's creative reputation. Deutsch LA was fast-becoming known for standout Super Bowl creative, like Mini-Darth and The Barkside for Volkswagen. More than that, in this case, an excellent showing in the Super Bowl commercial could certainly help Deutsch LA's hopes of becoming Taco Bell's agency of record one day.

This commercial had to be – yes, *must* be, – great.

Into this environment is born an idea called a 60-second brand commercial. I already told you earlier in this book how many people touch a Super Bowl commercial. Now you can imagine how nervous those people are – on the agency side and the client side – as they're handling said commercial. All of these people will collectively shape it, give input on it and eventually approve it at the last hour possible to make the air date – and, believe me, it's always the last hour possible. If there were no deadline Super Bowl spots would never ship, I'm convinced, due to over-analysis-paralysis.

If you're a creative person, there inevitably comes a moment during this angst-filled journey where you wonder: *Why did I sign up for this?* To be sure, the highs of Super Bowl commercial-making are real high along the way, and that's fun; but the lows? Oh, the low moments. I've had my share. Picture yourself lying awake at 3am, as if you'd just jumped into a glacial stream in Iceland, on the coldest day, in the middle of winter, – you're *that* awake thinking about how the first edit you just saw from your creative team at 11pm, right before bed, was an incoherent, hi-definition, 60-second train wreck. This train wreck keeps playing over and over again in your mind in slow motion, as you think about what your next career might look like when they hand you your walking papers. Get the picture? How about editors kicking door jams in frustration as they fine-tune a commercial that's been recut to the tune of 200 times? Picture advertising agency creative people arguing like children and walking out of edit bays. And ad agency bigwigs sweating blood, sure that the agency creative folks are doing something irresponsible to the commercial and thus eliminating the agency's chance to win the Super Bowl Admeter and, maybe, the whole account. (Oh, account people, you of the constantly worried, untrusting ilk.)

And so, into this environment your idea embarks on a journey.

The destination: 60 seconds of fame, infamy or irrelevance. And this journey, to that 8-million-dollar media time slot, sometime during the 3rd quarter, will be a collaborative one by necessity; there is no other way.

Now, fast-forward to nearly the end of this process. You've already sworn to yourself that you'll retire after this one is over and become a fisherman on a remote island near Bora Bora; but you've made it to this point and you find yourself, somehow, against all odds, with a Super Bowl-worthy commercial. It's edited perfectly. The music is dead-on. It's all working just as you hoped – maybe better than you hoped. You see yourself being back-slapped and high-fived at the agency as your commercial takes the number one position in the USA Today Admeter (which rates the "best" Super Bowl commercials every year) and takes its place as one of the greatest commercials in Super Bowl history, right next to Lee Clow's Ridley-Scott-Directed "1984", for Apple. Ok, none of that is likely, but your mind does race ahead. It has to, or you'd give up because there's still more to overcome – legal issues, clearance issues etc. etc.. So you're almost there, right at the precipice of potential Super Bowl-commercial greatness, so you tell yourself.

There's just one problem. There's a better version of the commercial you could be airing. This was the case with "Viva Young", Deutsch LA's commercial for the 2013 Super Bowl.

There were scenes that were left on the cutting room floor because we (the agency) collectively decided they weren't funny enough, or could be offensive to someone in Pocatello, Idaho who likes to write complaint letters to companies. The agency is probably playing defense now, cutting scenes out that could make the difference between memorable and forgettable, buzz-worthy and buzz-less. In the case of "Viva Young", the scenes that were being cut were being cut for all the "right" reasons. After all, this was the Super Bowl and when you get it wrong on this stage, you've failed –

27

as an agency and as a brand - in front of the whole world. So, we were only doing what we thought was right given the situation. Problem is - and this happens a lot in advertising - we were beginning to take the funny, the edge and the memorable stuff right out of our own commercial.

Trust the process? Yeah, right.

If you're a young creative team in advertising, as my team was in this story, doing your first Super Bowl ad (most creatives never get to do one at all) at this moment, well, you're having trouble *trusting the process.* After all, they were watching their commercial, which told the story of a bunch of old folks escaping a retirement home and going out and partying like they were 19-year-old kids, go down the proverbial tubes. They had a very funny concept but all the funny stuff – that they felt would make it actually entertaining to watch geriatrics party like they were 19 – was the very stuff that had been taken out of the commercial.

It's at this moment I receive a call from one worried art director with a very reasonable request: Can we get those funnier scenes back in? This particular art director knows we've decided - for all the reasons I mentioned - to leave these scenes on the cutting room floor. Yet he's asking me, his Executive Creative Director, in desperation, to do something about it. And I want to. I want to get those scenes back in because it's a better cut. I want to do it, because what's the worst thing that can happen, the client will say "no" if the scene is too scary for them?

It's at this point I want to go rouge and be a full NP (non-collaborative person, in case you forgot what that means). I want to take the situation into my own hands and whisper in my client's ear. After all, I'm convinced the cut could be better. The client will like it better with those scenes back in, I tell myself. But if I did that, as easy as it would be, would that be collaborative? No, it would mean I'm not being a team player. We, as an agency, made a collective decision and it's my job to stick with the plan.

And if I did show my client another cut, with all the stuff I thought should be in there, would that be *trusting the process?* No, indeed it would not. It would also make me insubordinate and untrustworthy. So, my answer to that worried art director who believed his Super Bowl ad was being ruined? "The process will have a corrective effect", I reassured him. "Trust me. Let the client reintroduce these scenes". And I wasn't just trying to put him off – I really believed it – I believed the client would ask for these scenes back. What I was effectively saying is this: let the *process* reintroduce those scenes.

At this moment, the *process* dictated that the commercial must go to the client for approval, <u>without</u> these scenes. The clients knew what we shot, they were all there on the shoot, after all! And the clients we're going to ask where those scenes went. They were going to want to see them in the cut, if only to consider them. Heck, they paid for 'em. "Where the heck are they?", I can already hear them saying in my head.

I'm not sure that understandably-worried agency creative believed me at the time, as he dejectedly hung up the phone; but I had a hunch the process would assert itself in this situation.

Sure enough, the client's reaction to the commercial – sans the more edgy and funny scenes - was "meh". The client response was something to the effect, "Nice commercial, but this is the Super Bowl, why isn't funnier? Can you make it more memorable? Please make it more of both of those things because that's what we came to you guys!" Okay, Mr. Client. Thank you. Be back tomorrow with that cut and those very scenes we left on the edit room floor. No going around any one's back or for any nasty NP behavior either.

The rigor of the *process* did the work for us – I've found it almost always does. And most of those funny scenes did indeed make the cut, in the end, complete with one old man sticking his boob against

Above: One of the scenes that was cut, then reintroduced via "the process", from Taco Bell's 2013 Super Bowl commercial, "Viva Young". Now what red-blooded American doesn't enjoy seeing an old man press his boob against a restaurant window full of people?

the glass of a restaurant full of snobby foodies. (Gordy and Brian, if you're reading this you must be smiling, you incredibly talented weirdoes. Love you.)

Oh, and the commercial? Well, it did not replace "1984" as the greatest commercial in history. It did, however, earn the title of the commercial with the most social buzz in the 2013 Super Bowl, according to Mashable. It also was the most Tweeted-about commercial, according to Twitter.

But here's the real point: to collaborate in high-stress situations and not self-destruct with negativity and finger-pointing, to keep your collaborative effort harmonious and, most importantly, effective...

...Trust the Process.

7

IN OTHERS WE MUST TRUST

There can be no collaboration with other people without trust.

Without trust, we cannot feel safe sharing our idea for fear someone else will take credit for it. Without trust, we cannot accept that criticism of our idea is coming from a good place. Without trust, we can't let anyone else handle any part of bringing our idea to life for fear that they will ruin it.

This is a short chapter, because there's not a whole lot to say about this except that it's true. Trust breeds collaboration. And the implications of this reality are that you must ask yourself these questions:

Are the people I'm working with trustworthy? Is the organization trustworthy? Lastly, take a look in the mirror. Are you trustworthy?

If the answer to any of the above questions is "no", great collaboration that will lead to brilliant ideas is not possible.

At one point in my career, I had to make the hard decision to leave a job because I no longer believed the people were trustworthy. I discovered that no one had anyone's back, including mine. No one trusted anyone else enough to let people do their jobs. There was no trust and therefore no real collaboration. We were eating each other alive and, frankly, it was unnecessary and counterproductive, to say the least.

Once I recognized this, and it took time to accept that it was a reality, I knew my time at this particular agency was over, because the chances to do great things were over too. In the final analysis, the real issue was this: we were not a group that trusted each other, therefore we did not collaborate well and therefore the ideas were suffering.

The above situation was a case where I felt the organization was operating in an untrustworthy, and therefore, un-collaborative way. But an equally valid question for you – and for me – is, what about us? Are we trustworthy? Is our criticism of another person's idea coming from a good, constructive place? Can we be trusted with someone's idea – to defend it? Help it? Grow it?

Trustworthy people are natural-born collaborators. Fact is, people want to collaborate with them because, yes, they trust them. And consequently, if you're trustworthy, opportunities to collaborate with people constantly present themselves. You will find yourself highly desired and constantly working. You will find yourself a part of some big ideas, too, when door after door opens to you. After all, talented, trustworthy and truly collaborative people are in short supply.

8

RESPECT. JUST A LITTLE BIT

We've talked a lot about the need for trust – trust for the creative process itself and for the people involved in the process. But there's another essential ingredient in order to collaborate well with others: respect.

Just a little bit.

Ms. Franklin had it right. And while she wasn't singing about collaboration in the pursuit of brilliant creative ideas, indeed, without R-E-S-P-E-C-T, all collaborations are bound to fail.

Here's a true story to illustrate the point: A hot shot tech guy from a hot shot company joins a new tech startup with real potential, with dreams of one day going public. The new hot shot shows up for work with a big cattle hat (a big title) and maybe even some cattle too (talent). And why shouldn't he have a big ego? He came from another famous hotshot tech company and, well, even there he was real hot shot. He was hired, after all, to bring his hotshot wisdom to this fledgling tech company full of well-intentioned, if somewhat less-talented and unambitious, people.

Naturally, ready to make a big splash, Hot Shot takes every opportunity to drop his knowledge on his fellow employees, be they peers or subordinates. He comes in hot and heavy, making quick assessments of people he's barely met and taking every opportunity to "educate" the people around him. He even offers some people unsolicited career advice. Hot Shot knows what's right for the fledgling tech startup, the product they're making, and knows what the consumer wants and needs, even though he's only been there a week. Hot Shot probably even means well, and he probably was even told by the big boss that this is what the company really needs, a real hotshot like Hot Shot who can shake things up.

Suddenly, Hot Shot finds people avoid his glance in the hallway. And just lately, he notices people seem to be busy every time he asks anyone to grab some lunch with him. People seem a little short around him and no one seems very open to his brave and fresh thinking. What's up with this company, he wonders? Bunch of non-collaborative people, Hot Shot thinks.

Fast-forward to six months later, Hot Shot discovers he's suddenly persona non grata at the company. Even the boss, who formerly thought Hot Shot was the cat's meow, now wonders why no one seems to want to collaborate on any projects involving Hot Shot. All this is really a bad development, because Hot Shot was a super expensive hire and he's not really panning out for the boss, which makes the boss's decision look really bad to the company leaders.

Sadly, but predictably, Hot Shot flames out at the fledgling tech company. Hot Shot is stumped. He doesn't really know why it happened. But the rest of the company does: Hot Shot didn't show any R-E-S-P-E-C-T to the people who bled, sweated and built that fledgling start-up. That's what happened, plain and simple.

We've all seen a version of this story in our own workplaces, and the point is simple:

When people don't feel respected, people will not collaborate.

Think about your most collaborative creative relationships; relationships with other individuals where things just "clicked". Part of it was the shared sensibilities and vision, to be sure, but part of it was definitely the feeling of mutual respect. Now think about your more dysfunctional, non-collaborative relationships. What was missing from them? If your scrape away the more superficial issues of differences in sensibilities etc., which, of course are real factors, deep beneath those things there was probably a sense that you – and your input – weren't respected by the other person.

Conversely, perhaps some of those people you never could collaborate well with thought you didn't respect them. Look, we've all been on both sides of the coin when it comes to respect and collaboration. I've certainly looked back at certain relationships and wondered if, perhaps, I came on too strong... too certain of my own opinions and too dismissive of the other person's ideas and input. Let's be honest, there's a little NP (non-collaborative person) lurking in all of us and we all have to watch that we're respecting others if we want to be excellent collaborators.

On the positive side, when respect is felt by people, great collaboration naturally follows. When you feel heard, dignified and see your ideas being woven into the tapestry of what's being created, there is nothing more invigorating and rewarding. Usually, when people are working with high-levels of mutual respect between each other, the ideas just flow and get better and better. Your confidence to speak from your gut goes up. Your willingness to throw out even stupid, half-baked thoughts goes up, because you feel it's safe to do so. And it's these half-baked, intuitive thoughts that are often where some brilliance is hiding. When respect is there, you feel free to fail and free to even look stupid, because underneath it all, you feel your input is valued. This is when collaborative efforts reach peak levels and amazing ideas take shape – and respect is the building block for it all.

Great collaborators respect other people and other people feel it, respond to it and usually return it. And let me tell you another little secret, when people feel you respect them, not only will they readily collaborate with you, they can be *influenced* by you. Respect is leverage, because when people see that you think highly of them, they'll do just about anything to make sure you continue to feel that way. When someone else remarks on a particular talent you possess, doesn't that make you want to live up to the compliment? We're all influenced by people who have put a lot of faith in what we bring to the table.

Let's bring the issue of respect and collaboration back to my particular business: advertising. The one thing that can unwind a client relationship faster than a bad piece of work or a major billing mistake, is a lack of respect. When clients feel their agency doesn't respect their input, even though the agency may be hired for their expertise and even though they may do great work, it's a quick way to lose the account. Conversely, the same is true for clients who don't show respect to the agency experts they've hired. When agencies don't feel respected by the client, the incentive to work hard on behalf of the client goes down. "What's the point, the client doesn't listen to us anyway", is a familiar refrain heard in agency hallways everyday. What that really means is: the client doesn't respect us.

Respect is the lifeblood of collaboration. Have a little R-E-S-P-E-C-T for others.

Just a little bit will go a long way towards better collaboration.

9

THE EMPATHETIC
SHALL INHERIT THE EARTH

One of my best friends, Victor Camozzi, who also happens to be a Group Creative Director at Ad Agency, GSD&M, in Texas, once said to me that our job, as creative leaders, all comes down to one thing: empathy.

I think his insight is profound as it relates to collaborating well with others in the pursuit of creating brilliant ideas. Let me explain why.

First, what is empathy anyway? Without looking it up, I'd say the definition is this: being able to see things from another person's point of view.

As it applies to the business of advertising, we need empathy to succeed on every level. First, we need to be able to empathize with the consumer and understand clearly what they want or need and how they view our product or service in relation to that want or need.

But we also need empathy in terms of understanding what our client's aims are, their ambition and goals. Then, as an agency, we must conceive creative solutions designed to meet the needs of both the consumer and the client, all while trying to achieve another aim: great conceptual creative work. We have to be able to see all points of view in order to envision a great creative solution. Empathy, the ability to understand other people – whose goals, perceptions and desires may be different from our own – is what the business of advertising is all about. I imagine any organization or business that seeks to provide a service or product to human beings must be empathetic in the end to succeed (with the exception of the California DMV... sorry, couldn't resist).

Empathy, as it applies to collaboration, is no different. It's the ability to see an idea from another person's point of view. By the way, I'm not even suggesting you need to agree with the POV. I am suggesting, however, that good collaborators CAN CLEARLY SEE THE IDEA FROM ANOTHER PERSON'S POINT OF VIEW – agree or disagree.

Are you capable of doing this? If you can't empathize with others' POVs, I'm convinced you can't be a good collaborator.

The next time your client, co-worker or boss says something you think is stupid, stop, and really think about what they're saying. Do you really understand what they just said, first of all. If not, ask for more clarity, ask them to expand on their thought and get them talking. The more you hear them talk, frankly, the more you can be sure of what their POV really is. You may discover you actually didn't really understand what they were saying at all. Or, maybe, after hearing them speak more about it, you'll realize that you do, indeed, understand his or her POV. That's good to know too.

Next, now that you have a better grip on what they really think, really consider what they said. Put yourself in that person's shoes. Think about their concerns regarding the idea. See it from their perspective. Really, sincerely, try to do this. Why do they think what they think? Why are they saying what they're saying? Do they really just want to make your life miserable or are they actually expressing a legitimate perspective, even if you don't totally agree?

The above sounds obvious and it is. Yet what do we usually do when we get creative feedback – especially feedback that seems off-based or wrong-headed initially? Our pulse rises. We get frustrated. We begin forming a defense of our own perspective before the person has even finished speaking. We stop listening, stop empathizing and simply look for the next moment to push our agenda. Sound familiar?

At times, we all do this because, frankly, it's the natural thing to do. It's the default setting of the human heart. And while it's an instinctual thing to do, it's certainly not empathic, nor will it enable brilliant collaboration.

Empathy is power. After all, to get another person to change their mind and see an idea your way – client or partner or employee – the best way to do it is via empathy for their POV. Especially clients, if they don't hear you expressing out loud, back to them, their POV about a particular idea, I absolutely promise they'll stop your agenda in its tracks. Why? Because it'll be clear that you can't see the problem from where they sit and if you can't do that, then you can't be making an informed, wise decision, because you don't understand the reality of the problem as they see it. It's that simple.

I can't tell you how many creative people are terrible at empathizing. They don't know how to play back or paraphrase back to another person, what they heard them say in a fair and objective way. They don't try to understand what other people are saying. They're too busy trying to win the argument or they're too convinced the client, co-worker or boss is stupid – or conversely, that their idea is right – to even attempt to empathize with the other person's POV. In fact, I've seen many creative people – rather than empathize, endeavor to showcase the stupidity of another person's thinking – they get some satisfaction out of it. Unfortunately, they also rarely win an argument about an idea ever – at least not without making enemies and often setting their own agendas (and careers) back in the process.

Empathy = credibility when it comes to collaboration.

In the end, good empathizers are incredibly hard to say no to. They make you feel heard. They demonstrate that they understand your POV. Therefore, you trust them more and you want to do what *they* want to do more. Good empathizers don't always win the argument and may not always be able to sway another person, but their credibility as good collaborators goes up exponentially because they demonstrate an understanding of other people's points of views.

I know what you're thinking: don't strong leaders "push back" and confidently shoot down other people's bad thinking? Won't I appear weak if I consider other people's points of view, particularly when the idea they're asking me to consider stinks?

No.

In fact, empathize consistently and I promise you, far from appearing weak, you'll become an incredibly strong voice that is able to lead others – clients, employees and partners – in the direction you'd like to take the idea.

And as far as collaboration in the pursuit of brilliant ideas is concerned, isn't that the goal?

10

KILL THAT BIG, FAT EGO

This one may be hard to swallow, but it's true: to really collaborate well, you're going to have to kill your big, fat ego.

That's a tough one for most creative types (it's tough for most human beings, for that matter), because whatever gene switches on when creative people are conceived seems to also switch on the big, fat ego gene. In my mind's eye I see thousands of advertising account people, the ones who must deal with creative people daily, nodding in agreement.

In any case, a big, fat ego will ruin any chance you have to be collaborative. How? Let us count the ways.

The ego wants to be right more than it wants the right idea.

I've seen this so many times, people holding on to an idea or being unwilling to change an idea, because, they need to be right. Clients who want to hold on to an old, boring idea because they gave birth to it and can't bear to admit they were wrong. Creative people who can't let go of a lame idea despite all the evidence it stinks. Chief Marketing Officers who blow up perfectly good, effective campaigns because they didn't create said perfectly good, effective campaigns. You see, the ego wants to be right more than it wants the right idea to win out, and this hurts collaboration and kills good ideas.

Ego leads to jealousy. Jealousy stops collaboration.

Then there's the flipside of having to be right: some people just want you to be wrong. That's ego. And that's its ugly, collaboration-killing step-child, jealousy.

What a collaboration-killing emotion, jealousy. Because of it, we find ourselves actually rooting for our co-workers – and sometimes – even our friends to NOT succeed. Ever found yourself doing this? I've certainly caught myself in the act. Boy, it's an ugly impulse. We sometimes even let our jealousy get in the way of someone helping us make an idea better – for fear that someone else might get the credit, or because we think we should figure it all out ourselves. Now that's just plain stupid. That's against our own interests and the best interests of the idea, but it happens all the time thanks to our big, fat ego.

The ego says, "My ideas are always better."

I feel bad for people who think their ideas are always better. They create so much extra work for themselves. While they may even be right, that indeed many times their ideas are best, they miss so many thoughts, suggestions and embellishments that could make their idea better or even lead them to a whole new brilliant idea.

Maybe I'm just lazy, but I'm all ears when it comes to hearing a way to make an idea better or entertaining a new idea. They can come from anywhere and anyone, if you're listening. They make your life easier. They take some of the load off your shoulders because you no longer have to try and solve it all. Furthermore, you can always reject a bad idea, so what's the harm in allowing others to offer you their opinions, thoughts and ideas?

People with small egos are not threatened by other people's opinions. They know that other people can make their idea better. Is your ego small enough to make room for others' ideas? If not, you're just making your own job harder and your own, prized ideas, weaker.

The Benefits of a Small Ego

I like to think I have a pretty manageable ego (how egotistical of me to say that!) Oh, to be sure, my ego rears its ugly head on occasion. And like most people, my ego wants me to be recognized, it wants me to be the hero of the big meeting, to be the guy with the grand idea. Yes, my ego wants all of those things, just like everyone else. But somewhere along the way, I learned that a big, fat ego would only lead to a lot of frustration, enemies and disappointment.

You see, there aren't enough accolades or praise or recognition to ever fill your big, fat ego. I found mine just wants more no matter how much I feed it. Someone compliments you or you're recognized for something and your ego feels satiated for a moment. Then, soon after, it gets hungry again, looking for another heaping helping of compliments, accolades and recognition.

Besides the problem of there never being enough compliments and recognition for big, fat egos, who really enjoys working with, much less being around, other egotistical people? Let's face it, humility is a really attractive quality. We seek it out in other people.. Humble people have lots of friends and lots of people who want to work with them. Humble people with small egos instantly remove so many of the barriers to collaboration because they are so obviously focused on ideas, not themselves.

Yes, a small disciplined ego has so many benefits when it comes to collaborating in the pursuit of brilliant ideas. It allows other people to make you better. It allows you to see others' ideas as worth listening to – and this will make you more successful than you could be on your own. It helps you to see things from other people's perspectives – this strengthens your ideas because it means you've inspected them and vetted them from every angle.

Keeping my ego in check – while a daily struggle and not easy (I've certainly failed many times) has allowed me to collaborate well. In fact, it might be the single greatest reason I've been fortunate to have a rewarding career as a creative person. I say this because I readily admit there are plenty of people who are much more talented than me. Some of these talented people, though, are terrible collaborators working on the fringes of the advertising world. I'm sure you know of situations like this in your own industry. Their names pop up and you say to yourself, what ever happened to that guy?

One of the things I'm constantly doing is this: I make a conscious effort to really examine the real motives behind my actions as I'm collaborating with others, especially when I'm having a problem. In these situations, I truly try to see it from the other person's point of view. When I examine my motives honestly, I often catch myself contributing to situations where collaboration is breaking down. Also, I've found it helps to have a trusted friend to get another perspective about these situations, someone who knows you really well. For me, those people are my wife and mother, who are often quick to point out when I am letting my ego and pride get in the way. Who might that person be for you?

Staying humble, examining your own motives when collaboration breaks down, and getting an outside perspective are all excellent ways to help kill that big, fat ego. I promise if you do, you, your ideas and your overall career, will benefit.

By the way, there's a fringe benefit: when you kill that big, fat ego, you're going to be happier too.

Other people are going to be happy for you when you succeed, as well.

11

THE SPECIAL
CHALLENGE OF BIG IDEAS

Above: Taco Bell's campaign for their new breakfast, which featured real people, named Ronald McDonald from across America, professing their love for Taco Bell's breakfast.

There's an old saying: Success has many fathers. Failure is an orphan. It's an instructive saying and one that I've found to be very true.

I've seen work I've been a part of fail, only to discover I'm suddenly standing pretty much alone with the wreckage at my feet.

Where did all those people go that were once a part of this big idea? On the other hand, I've been a part of some big ideas that suddenly have fathers – and mothers – all claiming custody, seemingly from out of nowhere.

The point I want to make here is this: big, hairy ideas – even half-formed big, hairy ideas – will present a special challenge when it comes to collaborating well with others. Why? Because big ideas make careers. Big ideas make people famous. Big ideas make for big raises. Therefore big ideas bring out egos, territorialism, distrust and fear – in other words, all the worst parts of people and all of the usual suspects that threaten to undo collaboration.

It's hard enough to expose our bad ideas to other people, much less our big, hairy ones. When we have big ideas, all the same threats to collaboration come into play, ONLY NOW THEY'RE ON STERIODS.

Once upon a time, I was the lucky custodian of one of those big, hairy ideas. I helped create it, shape it and sold it to the client. I poured myself into making this idea great. As it began to take shape and come to fruition, I found that all kinds of people suddenly had opinions about it. Some of these people were not all that involved at any point in imagining or making this idea, but that's not stopping them from offering lots of opinions now, as it comes into its final stages. And these people, while not ill-intentioned, are not really helping me or the idea either. In my opinion, at times, they're even muddling the process. They're actually causing needless overthink.

We've all been in this situation. So, what to do? How can you collaborate when you're holding a big idea and people – people with the power to do so - want to change it, shape it, put their name on it or just jump on the 'ole bandwagon? This is a hard one, isn't it? It's so easy to become paranoid, defensive or aggressive in this situation – it's easy to become a jerk and help kill your career when you think you have a big idea.

First thing, recognize what's going on and congratulate yourself. You're quite possibly onto something big if you see lots of people coming out of the woodwork with a desire to collaborate on this "big" idea. I'm being a little facetious here, but honestly, it's about having some perspective in moments like these. If what's driving people to want to be part of your idea is the obvious potential of it, step back and recognize this and celebrate it.

This is a good thing, after all.

Big ideas are very hard to come by.

Second, remember that though your idea may be big, you're going to need help to make it real, and if nothing else, better. Yes, you are going to need people – people with expertise you may not have - to help you make your idea great. Don't be that guy that goes to his grave with the better mousetrap, but was too paranoid to let others help him build it. You must remember that letting other people offer opinions about your idea, letting them shape it even, this is the reality of *the process* of bringing concepts to life. And we already talked about having *trust in the process* (this is where that "trusting the process" stuff really gets tested).

When you find yourself needing to collaborate with people on your big idea – by necessity – see it as an excellent way to find out the truth about your big idea. Are lots of people struggling with some key part of the idea? Maybe that part should be eliminated or altered in some way. Do lots of people really like a particular aspect of the idea? Maybe that can be accentuated or perhaps that "really liked" aspect can be applied in more places etc. There is wisdom in the masses – not always, of course – but often there are bits of truth that can only be unearthed with collective wisdom. So, open yourself and your big idea to some of that wisdom.

Be willing to share your big idea, but never park your passion.

Third, while you need to be open to points of view on your big idea, remember to never park your passion. As your big idea journeys from your head to the real world, the many opinions it will confront will indeed impact its ultimate shape and form. As the main steward of your big idea, it's your obligation to also use your gut to guide it to its best manifestation. Remember, if you're a good collaborator – respectful, open and secure –your voice is a powerful factor in the ever-evolving *process*. While respect and trust for others is critical, asserting your vision at key points in your idea's journey is critical too. We've all looked back at certain times in our careers and marveled at a key decision that was "make or break" in terms of a particular concept. Having the wisdom to recognize these junctures and having the courage to stand up for your convictions regarding your big idea, is critical.

It's *how* you do this that will make the difference. And the key to defending your ideas successfully is doing it with *passion*.

I've found people almost never object to passion when discussing an idea. Quite the opposite, they're drawn to it. What else explains the cult of personalities out there like Steve Jobs, Richard Branson or advertising legend, Lee Clow? These people, above all else, have demonstrated incredible passion for ideas. When you're passionate about an idea, people listen. When you're passionate, people rarely take offense at your comments or criticisms because they sense you're coming from an authentic place. When you're passionate, people realize you're simply out to do the best thing for the idea, not the best thing for yourself.

Don't be stingy with the credit.

Lastly, when you've successfully launched a big idea, try to be liberal with the credit. Here's why: first, people truly appreciate being credited, even if their contribution to the big idea was smaller than your own. Second, you would want, and would also appreciate, a little credit if you contributed to another person's big idea in a tangible way. Third, we all tend to overestimate our own contributions to ideas and forget the critical contributions of others, so be careful to not leave people off the credits list because you've failed to really appreciate what someone brought to the table on a particular project.

Finally, if the idea of a laundry list of names going on your big idea frustrates you, remember, if you're a talented creative person, there's more great work that you'll be a part of – talented and collaborative people are rarely just great once. This last part is important because you will be judged by your body of work, not just by one idea (I don't know about you, but I want to be a consistent hitter, not a one hit wonder when it comes to ideas). You don't want to get so territorial and egotistical in an effort to get more or all of the credit, that you alienate others by leaving them off the credits. After all, your big idea will one day, sadly, be just another idea that has come and gone, replaced by some other big idea. Don't burn career bridges by being stingy about credit.

And let's say by chance, that sure-fire, big idea – that one that was sure to take the world by storm – were to turn out to be a failed, orphan-of-an idea in the end? Well, collaborative people, who played nice and let others into the process along the way, who shared credit liberally, have in effect "shared" the culpability for the idea. If the big idea does fail – and some big ideas just do – it's more likely to be viewed as collective/organizational failure, than a personal one. Whereas if you've alienated others on the way to making your big idea, and then, it fails… well, you will discover the real meaning of "Failure is an orphan". And your failed idea won't be the only orphan, you're sure to be one too, all alone, standing with the wreckage of your big idea at your feet wondering, *where is everybody?*

To close, remember that big idea I mentioned earlier, the one people came out of the woodwork for and wanted to be a part of? Well, the idea did turn out to be a doozy. And yes, some folks jumped on the credit wagon when it turned out to be a winner. Yes, lots of fathers and mothers showed up to this particular waiting room to claim some ownership of the success of this big idea. Some folks had legitimate claims, others perhaps not so much, at least in my judgment. (I wish there was an intellectual DNA test for certain spurious claims on creative ideas.) The latter lost credibility with some of their co-workers and I think they'll be sculpting in their garage at some point if they continue with that sort of behavior – it always catches up with people. As for me, I'd rather play nice and let others just expose themselves – which they will over time - for who they are. After all, people recognize an NP when they see one.

In the end, collaborative people are adept at handling the special challenges presented by big ideas. They know how to defend big ideas, let their co-workers and superiors help them improve them, they use their passion to help protect their ideas along the way and they liberally credit others that help them shape it – all without letting the promise of potential fame and fortune – which is fleeting anyway - that *could* come from the big idea, poison the collaborative process.

12

CREDIT PEOPLE. PUBLICLY

We talked a bit about how much people like to be credited and the value of being liberal in giving that credit.

If you want to encourage collaboration, here's another thing to add to the notion of giving credit to people: do it publicly.

People love getting credited for their contributions, but people *really* love it when you do so publicly.

We've already noted that your influence grows – as does your ability to navigate your idea through the process - when people see that you are a collaborative person who dignifies others' input. Your influence will grow even more when people see that you go out of the way to publicly point out people's contribution to their co-workers and their bosses.

When people see you do this, it's a massive deposit towards

achieving great collaboration. Who doesn't love to have their contribution to an idea celebrated – and celebrated publicly? Who doesn't remember those moments? Who doesn't grow more loyal to the people who recognize them publicly? In an environment where people's contributions are recognized publicly, people feel valued and energized. They see that the company and its leaders don't take their contributions for granted. They see that there is a commitment to intellectual honesty when big ideas are hatched, shaped and brought to life.

When people are given credit publicly, people don't guard their big ideas, they share them with the confidence that their contribution will be fairly noted and properly celebrated.

Public recognition can be done in small and big ways. It's everything from a quick mention in a meeting such as, "Helen had a great idea...", to a simple email, to getting up in front of the whole company and telling everyone what someone did.

Make this a habit, and trust, loyalty and your influence will grow. And most importantly, you'll make brilliant collaboration not only possible, but inevitable.

13

NEVER SAY "I TOLD YOU SO"

There's a deadly set of words that damages collaboration in the pursuit of brilliant ideas: told you so. It's when ego asserts itself and we feel the need to let others know we were right about our hunch, our choice, our ideas.

Like most advertising writers and art directors, I attended a school, post-graduation, that helped me learn how to think conceptually. In this school, like most advertising creative schools, you are partnered with other people. It's a good exercise since advertising has a standard, long-practiced approach of pairing an art director with a copywriter. This is the first time I truly experienced collaboration with another person in the pursuit of ideas. It would be the model for how I would need to work for the next decade in ad agency world.

The way these advertising school classes were structured, we'd get an assignment to make up some faux ads on behalf of a brand our instructor would randomly designate. An example would be, "Create a billboard for Jeep's new Wrangler". Our instructor would then ask us to present our ideas to the entire class. What he would be analyzing is both the strategic insight behind our idea and the creative execution. The process of learning to effectively concept great advertising was like learning to ride a bike: you have to crash a few times to be able to competently ride down the street – only in these classes you did so publicly, in front of dozens of other insecure, aspiring creative people.

Naturally, there was some pressure – pressure to solve the problem, pressure to present well and pressure to impress the instructor and your peers. And amidst all of this, I'm learning how to do all of the above with a partner. While a partner is very helpful in coming up with ideas, the productiveness of the partnership really depends on the partnership itself – the chemistry and the fit of the two people. That would seem obvious, but it's especially true in regards to creative teams in advertising.

I was the writer and my partner was an art director. Turns out we had zero chemistry. For my part, I was an insecure, "regular Joe" from the working-class San Fernando Valley. My new partner, on the other hand, was from an artsy-fartsy part of town and looked like the lead singer of The Doors – good looking, pony-tailed and wearing leather pants. All this and I don't think he even played in a band. It left this valley boy feeling a little intimidated.

When I threw out ideas to my partner for our assignments, I felt like I was telling Prince how he might play the guitar. Besides being almost totally unfruitful in terms of any good ideas, our partnership made me question whether I was just a hack that needed to find a new career path. Of course, I assumed I was the problem in the equation. That's just my personality.

In any case, mostly what the two of us did when we were

together is stare at each other and sit in uncomfortable silence. And the longer it would go on, the more unnerving it became. As it turns out, bad partnerships happen all the time in advertising, but since it was my first time, I had no perspective or experience to comfort me.

As we approached the first presentation of our ideas for our homework assignment, I had some apprehension. Our concepts were average and my partner and I didn't agree on almost anything about them. But like real agency life, the presentation must go on – complete agreement or not. You must still present your idea as a united front – that's the way it is in advertising.

About five minutes into our presentation of an ad with a talking Jeep (I'm making this up but I'm sure the idea stunk), our instructor offers a thought on what we could've done to make it better. What does my partner do in response? He decides to call me out in front of the whole class. He turns to me and says, "I told you we should have done that", or something to that effect. And indeed, he may well have told me exactly what the instructor said we should have done with the idea and I probably was wrong, but the point is, that wasn't exactly the most collaborative thing to do.

I remember thinking, wow, what a jerk. And what poor judgment. I didn't know a lot about what a good partnership looked like, but somewhere up towards Rule No. 1 had to be: Don't blame your partner, when an idea goes over poorly, in front of a crowded room of people.

Besides being an immature thing to do, my young partner fell into the trap, that sets back all collaborative efforts, of needing to point out that he was right. We ALL have done this. We all feel the need, by virtue of our ever-present ego, to let people know we were right, or, conversely, that they were wrong.

Resist the temptation!

NEVER SAY "I TOLD YOU SO".

Let's face it, the reality of collaborating on ideas is this: not all steps are forwards. On the way to conceiving something great, ideas often go backwards, stall, or meander off the path. This is all part of the process of discovering the true potential of an idea. The last thing you want to have happen is to have people fear making a suggestion because it may one day be thrown back in their face if it all goes wrong. Together, you collectively mold it as best you can and if there's a set-back with a client or superior, you just accept the challenge, adjust and move on. No need for recrimination or reminders of how this person or that person didn't "get it" or "should've listened to you".

Many times in my advertising career clients or my bosses have resisted my creative recommendations, only to later see that, in the end, I had it right. But what would I gain if I reminded them I was right? Not much. In fact, they might conclude I was becoming an egotistical jerk and they'd probably be right. Also, just as often, I've been wrong. Would I want that fact thrown back in my face?

The truth is, nobody wants to collaborate with people who need to constantly point out how "right" they were about something. On the other hand, people love collaborating with those who can compliment someone for their good judgment in regards to shaping and molding an idea.

DO SAY "YOU WERE RIGHT".

While it's never beneficial to point out to others that *you* were "right", it is highly beneficial to collaboration to admit to others when *they* were "right". This is an act of humility, but it's one that goes a long way with people – provided they're not an NP. Every so often, it's worth going out of your way to acknowledge a peer's, subordinate's, even a boss's "rightness" about a particular idea that you may have initially disagreed with. I choose to see those moments as opportunities to make a "deposit" into the relationship I have with that person. Saying "You're right", says you're not ego-driven, but idea-driven. It also shows clearly that you are cognizant of others' contributions to the idea and willing to say so.

In the end, saying "I told you so" will kill collaboration and collaborative relationships. Occasionally saying "you were right" will foster even greater collaboration.

14

EXCUSES TO
AVOID COLLABORATION

We humans, when we don't want to do something, are very adept at creating rationalizations for our behavior.

And make no mistake, we often don't want to collaborate. It's hard, after all. It means opening our ideas up to criticism. It means having to defend our thinking. It means having to genuinely consider other points of view.

If collaboration were easy and if it came naturally, I wouldn't be writing this book and you wouldn't be reading it. The excuses we use to avoid collaboration are myriad, but ultimately, they're just that: excuses.

Let's take a look at some of the excuses we use to avoid the one thing that can consistently make us – and our ideas – better.

I won't get all the credit if I collaborate with others.

It's true, if you bring others into the effort of shaping and ultimately achieving your idea, other people's names are going to go on the trophy, if you're indeed successful. Why does that stop people? Because our ego wants to be recognized - plain and simple.

But let me ask you, would you rather not ever see your idea come to life at all? Let's be honest, as we discussed earlier, even Steve Jobs couldn't make an iPhone all by himself. He may have had a vision, but he most definitely did not have all the means. He needed people. All great ideas start in someone's head and then, 99% of the time, they need people (notice the plural) to make them great and, more importantly, real.

I'm not suggesting you don't use discretion in how you share ideas and with whom, this requires wisdom on your part. But letting others in on the thought – which is all an idea is in the beginning – is an unavoidable part of making it real.

Other People Will Ruin my Idea if I Collaborate.

It's true, other people could ruin your idea. Then again, you could ruin your own idea by not sharing it. How? By not seeing how your idea is being perceived and received by others. By not beating up the idea a little bit with other smart people, which shows the cracks in the veneer or, conversely, shows that indeed your idea may hold water. Or you could ruin any chance of your idea coming to life by holding it so close to the vest that it dies with you and is buried six feet under, never to see the light of day. Many great ideas die this way, I'm convinced.

I don't like collaborating with people who aren't "at my level".

Some people reach a certain level in their careers where they no longer want to collaborate with people junior to them. It's a somewhat understandable impulse. After all, we all want to collaborate with the people that excite us, challenge us, and those people are often our equals and those senior to us. Besides, we all understand instinctively that we must collaborate with those senior to us, because not doing so could damage our careers. These "senior" people sign our paychecks, after all, so collaborate we must. People that are junior to us are a different story entirely. These people are often less experienced, have no authority over us and, frankly, do not sign our checks, so it's easy to think that one need not collaborate well with people "beneath" them.

If we hold the attitude that people less senior are not worth collaborating with and can't help our ideas, we miss yet another resource that could make our idea better. Often these "junior" people are younger and more connected to culture and technology. They see things in different ways – ways that could help make your idea more contemporary, vibrant and relevant – and great ideas are always highly relevant.

I know excellent creative minds whose ego forbids them from collaboration with people junior to them. Not only do they miss out on a fresh, youthful perspective, the people they refuse to work with also largely resent them. These people are not well-liked, they are not seen as collaborative and the moment they fail, they will find themselves alone.

The simple truth is, if you won't collaborate with anyone less senior than you, you're sending a message that you do not respect that person. People tend to resent people that don't pay them any respect, last time I checked.

I'm not suggesting you throw pearls before swine, but I am suggesting you don't exclude those that are less senior simply for being so. Finally, those people beneath you, often end up above you, in your chosen industry – I've seen this many times. Why prematurely close that finite career window, in which you have the chance to make your ideas come to life, by making people dislike you?

15

THE HIGHER YOU GO

Not long ago, I promoted two enormously talented creative people who, at times, struggled with collaborating well with others. They were now going to be Associate Creative Directors, which in Advertising lingo means you will direct others' ideas, but you will also still be taking direction from superiors above you as well. It's a very tricky, political and incredibly challenging position, but one that is necessary if you're ever to become a full-fledged creative director charged with overseeing the overall creative direction of a brand.

Since my two, newly promoted guys were not natural collaborators, I reminded them that in their new role they would need to be MORE collaborative, not less. I'm not sure what they thought of that, but in my own career it's proven to be true.

Ironic, isn't it? The notion that the higher we climb in our careers the more collaborative we must become? If you can't grasp this idea, you'll stymie your career growth.

I mentioned this role of Associate Creative Director in

Advertising, the transitional phase all art directors and copywriters who aspire to lead must pass through if they're to become true creative leaders. I imagine that other creative industries have a similar position – you are tasked with developing other people's creative ideas, yet you must also take direction yourself from creative people above you. Let's call it middle management, because that's basically what it is.

In terms of collaboration, middle management can be a very tricky path to negotiate. For instance, some of the people who report to you will see you as a layer between them and the "real" decision makers above you. This also happens from the other direction as your boss may often leap you to give direction directly to the people below you. All this can lead to some real frustration as your direction is constantly challenged from below and sometimes reversed from above, making you feel like just a layer in a 7-layer dip indeed.

It's at this point you may find yourself wondering if you've actually taken a step backwards in your career, because you neither directly create the raw ideas anymore, nor do you have final say on how they turn out. This is a vexing development, because you thought being promoted meant – more than ever – you get to call the shots. And in a sense, you do – at least more of them. But while you may have more seniority and the mandate to shape other people's ideas, you now realize what you really must do is be an extraordinary collaborator, a person who can motivate others below you and gain their respect, yet know when to get out of the way when your boss steps into the picture to offer guidance.

I found very few creative people make the transition to middle management well because they don't know how to deal with these collaborative challenges. Often, they're annoyed when their subordinates challenge their creative direction, letting their insecurity over not being the "final say" in the process get to them. They see pushback from their art directors and copywriters on an idea as blatant disrespect – and sometimes it is; yet a lot of times pushback and disagreement is just healthy dialogue that should be encouraged, not stifled. It's how ideas get better, after all.

Conversely, many creative people in middle management get defensive when their creative director offers a suggestion of any kind, feeling their authority/control over their people – and the idea – has been subverted. Sometimes bosses do micromanage and overstep their roles and treat middle management folks like a layer; but just as often, as a middle manager, your insecurities come into play and you forget that the reason you even have superiors is because these people can often make you smarter, your idea better and ultimately help you succeed in the process.

Yet it's not just middle management leaders who must be great collaborators. It's the more senior leaders too. In fact, they must be and often are, the best collaborators of all.

Let's return to my advertising example. In our industry, your next step up after Associate Creative Director, should you chose to accept this mission, will be to become a Creative Director. Now you're really a big shot who gets to tell people what to do, right? You get to be less collaborative now, right? Now you get to be Kim Jong Il Junior, and just tell everyone how their idea should be – after all, it's your little creative-dictatorship-of-a-world now, right?

Wrong.

Sure, now you can act like a big, narcissistic jerk if you like. The only trouble is, you won't last long as a creative leader. You'll be sculpting in your garage soon, wondering how your career went wrong just when you were promoted. What happened? You're an award-winning, genius creative director, after all.

You acted like a non-collaborative jerk. That's what happened.

Leadership requires that people actually want to follow you.

Without people following behind you, leading is kind of, well, tough. And in order for people to want to follow you, you must be an extraordinary collaborator. So as a creative director – or any kind of senior leader in any creative industry – while you may not be a layer in a middle management sandwich anymore, you now must get the people in middle management to want to work for you and feel valued by you. You must also get the people who are further down the chain to want to follow you too.

So how do you do it?

By being judicious about when and where you leap your middle management's authority and direction to their subordinates. By listening to the counsel and advice your middle management folks give to you. By being willing to change your mind about an idea, and swallow your ego when your people make compelling arguments.

Middle management folks love working for bosses who validate them, dignify their thinking and allow for pushback and disagreement. And when you set this tone on your team, people not only feel empowered and valued, they impart the same feeling to the people below them. This makes everyone feel empowered, valuable and satisfied as they have a say in the creative process. This is how collaborative environments are formed, and if you're leader, you've got to set this collaborative tone – to be carried out down the line of your entire team – if you want a happy, productive team who can create brilliant ideas together.

But there's yet another way leaders are challenged to become more collaborative than ever as they move up the chain of influence: they must now collaborate brilliantly with other leaders in the organization. This is yet another challenge entirely, and one with its own unique set of hurdles.

Collaboration with those who are also charged with leading alongside you is fraught with potential pitfalls. One big one worth mentioning is Ego. Yes, Ego. And I'm not just talking about the other leader's ego, I'm talking about YOUR ego.

If you're a leader, you've grown accustomed to following your gut and you've most likely had a certain amount of success doing so. All of which means, you're more likely – at this stage in your career – to resent or, perhaps, question some other person telling you how you might make your idea better. After all, you've been put in the position you're in because of your ability to shape ideas, so why do you have to listen to anyone else now?

Yet you must listen, and here's why: some of these other leaders are actually smart and talented too (that's how they became leaders. Duh.) and often, if you're listening with an open mind, they can make your idea better. But even if you don't believe that, there's this: other leaders *expect* to be listened to, just as you do. They're more likely to feel confident that they have something valuable to offer, and, in fact, their position would indicate that this is indeed true. Yes, some people land in leadership who shouldn't, but many are equipped for the task on some level. In any case, these other leaders will expect to have their comments dignified and listened to – you can count on it. And since you're an ace collaborator, you don't need other leaders in your organization saying you're not open to input, because let's face it, these people have influence and are close to the seats of power too. You don't need other leaders as enemies, you need them as supporters and collaborators if you want to make brilliant creative ideas.

A final word on the need to be more collaborative the higher you go: in my career, I've had the opportunity to work with well-known CEOs and CMOs of some famous brands. What often strikes me about most of these people is that they're often the ones who listen the most in the meeting. They often can be influenced by those around them because they value the counsel of other smart people. They're open to respectful disagreement. They're geniuses at making the big decisions in a way that makes everyone feel like they've contributed to the final outcome. All of this is a by-product of something else I often see in these people: a sense of humility mixed with a genuine belief that other people have something to contribute to every idea. They believe other people can make their ideas, their products and services, better.

What I've found at the top of famous brands and companies like Taco Bell, Sony PlayStation, Activision and Dr Pepper, to name a few, are *brilliant collaborators*.

Wonder how these people got where they did?

16

COLLABORATE UP, DOWN AND SIDEWAYS

With so many challenges to collaborating to begin with, it's tempting to want to just ignore, step over or go around certain "junior" - or even "mid-level" clients - in the effort to make a great idea come to life. It's easy to listen respectfully to what the president of a company says – after all, they've got a ton of experience, they can sign checks, approve ideas, and they could fire you with a phone call. Obviously we all have less trouble (if only out of self-preservation) mustering the desire to collaborate with powerful, senior clients.

That said, I will let you in on a little secret: how you collaborate with your less-senior clients – almost always – will determine how good your relationship will be with your most-senior clients.

I've always made it a point to try to genuinely listen to concerns and comments from ALL of my clients – from the most senior ones, right down to the most inexperienced. I take notes, make eye contact and listen to everyone's opinion. Notice I said "listen", not necessarily "act" upon. After all, many of the comments blurted out in a meeting – particularly by the more inexperienced clients – are not worth pursuing or reacting to. But it's never a waste of time to listen to even what seems to be the silliest comment from the most junior client – sometimes those *silly* ideas end up being worthwhile ideas.

And remember, most junior and mid-level clients know what's on their senior boss's mind. Often, they are saying what the boss may not want to say or is too diplomatic to say; so you'd be wise to listen because you may be hearing the private angst and concern of your head client that would otherwise not surface. In fact, many times more senior clients like letting their direct reports surface concerns – concerns that are actually their own - because that way it lets them be the good cop. After all, they don't want to be constant killjoys for your grand creative ambitions (the good ones don't anyway), so they let someone else – their next in charge – be the bad cop. So listen up, you may be hearing more than just some junior client's opinion.

Another reason to learn to collaborate well with your junior and mid-level clients is that you will likely spend way more time rubbing elbows with them. They're in the trenches with you more as they are often far more "hands-on", while the president or CMO (Chief Marketing Officer) may only show up for the occasional important meeting. This means collaborating well with these people is even more important, because you'll be working with them constantly. They'll get the best sense of anyone as to what kind of collaborator you are – good or bad – and I'll promise you something: they will share those opinions with their bosses – the good and the bad.

I'm absolutely convinced that many client relationships sour from the bottom up. Conversely, strong client relationships are forged from the bottom up. After all, the president doesn't know what you're like to work with on a daily basis – she is too busy; but guess who she likely trusts and who knows exactly what you're like to collaborate with? Her less senior employees who work with you all the time. Believe me, they will talk to their bosses, and opinions – based on their perceptions - will be formed.

What are your clients – at all levels – saying about you? That you're a collaborative person or a nasty NP?

What your less senior clients say about your willingness to collaborate – or lack thereof – may have more to do with whether you will create great ideas, or for that matter, retain a client's business than almost anything else. If they're singing your praises to the President, it can be the one thing that saves you when something goes wrong – let's face it, in the business of creating ideas and products, things always go wrong. Conversely, it can be the thing that puts you over the edge when you put a big, scary idea in front of them and the client has to walk out on a ledge and trust you, because, well, this is a big, scary idea and it will take guts and massive amounts of trust capital to make it happen.

Speaking from personal experience, I've been blessed with incredibly solid client relationships over my career. And I got to thinking about the *why*. The answer to that is why I'm writing this chapter. The *why*, I'm convinced, is that I developed strong, collaborative relationships with senior clients, of course – but more importantly, I collaborated well with the junior and mid-level clients. There is no other explanation for it. How else do you have CMOs raving about your "relationship" when you've only physically sat in two meetings with them? (This has happened.) The answer is simple: the CMO's judgment was informed by their employees who actually work with you day in and day out.

When the clients like collaborating with you, good things happen – they become internal advocates for you, a sort of 5th column that supports your ideas when you're not even there to advocate for them. They are there at critical moments when an idea could die any one of the thousand deaths that are waiting for good ideas. Will they defend your idea and vision? If you collaborate well with them, I'm betting many times they will.

Let me give you an example. Once upon a time I did a brand commercial, what we commonly call an anthem, for Dr Pepper. They wanted an emotional launch commercial that would set up the new campaign idea. The concept for the commercial was simple: a film that celebrates one of a kind people, brought to you by the soda with a One of a Kind taste. Not complicated.

To help them envision the idea for this commercial, I did what we call a rip-o-matic film – an assemblage of found/pre-existing footage set to music. Every agency does these – and we do them often – as a way to help the client wrap their heads around an idea. To help sell the idea, I put a catchy, but in hindsight, bit too feel-good track to the rough picture.

Above: Dr Pepper's commercial for the launch of their one-of-a-kind brand campaign.

Of course, everyone fell in love with it, right up through the entire company.

When that happens, we call that "Demo Love", when people fall in love with the music or voiceover talent that's on the rip-o-matic film they keep watching and then no one can bear to see it or hear it any other way. It's a very easy trap to fall into.

Understand that this is a predicament (Demo Love) which is very common and very hard to undo. Also understand that this song was very uplifting, inclusive and sweet – the kind of track that's hard to quibble with, as there was nothing to *not* like about it. Yet on further reflection, the song seemed to lack a bit of swagger and wasn't as attention-getting as we wanted it to be. Still, Dr Pepper was quite happy with the demo music I put on the cut. I was enamored with it too, but we started to feel it wasn't as "modern" or "youthful" or "edgy" as we needed it to be.

So we, the agency, embarked on an effort to find a track that was more modern, edgy and youthful. But, of course, the leadership at Dr Pepper had already settled on the song we had shown them. As in, they were ready to buy the track. As in, they essentially told us: we are running that commercial with the song you have on it, because we love it. But now the agency is convinced we should move away from this music and I'm being pressured to find a new track.

What a pickle. This is going to be a headache – one that I created.

After putting what seemed like a million songs to picture, we finally found a fantastic new track by a French DJ team, known as C2C. It was a youthful, edgy, soon-to-be released track and the band itself was one of a kind. The song simply sounded like nothing any of us had ever heard and as the editor pressed play, we realized it drove the picture beautifully. With any luck, it would become a famous song and take the Dr Pepper brand along for the ride. That is, if we could get Dr Pepper to move away from the track we originally presented and instead approve the new one we had fallen in love with. The track we all thought was stronger.

As it turned out, I was soon to discover we had a secret weapon at our disposal – our clients themselves. Many of them, as it turned out, loved the song too when they saw it to picture. So much so that they began to believe, like us, that we ought to move to use the new one instead, despite the fact that there was consensus at the top of their company to stick with the original track.

But long before this situation occurred, we had developed a very positive, collaborative relationship with these clients. In other words, we had developed a deep level of trust and cooperation. And that, as it turned out, would make an otherwise impossible situation, possible.

To our collective surprise, we found our clients on fire to get the whole organization to approve the new song. They were canvassing the halls, writing emails, negotiating and securing rights to the track, formulating strategies – all with the intention of pushing this music through their own company.

The agency? We were doing pretty much nothing. At this point, it was all our clients. Imagine that, our clients were fighting as hard for the good ideas as we would ourselves. In fact, they were fighting harder than we possibly could. And with more credibility – the kind of credibility that could only come from them. And frankly, they could do what we could never do: negotiate the personalities, the various agendas, financial hurdles in the company and get us to the point where we really just needed a final approval from the CMO. We couldn't possibly do that since it would be too complicated and we simply don't have access to the key people nor the information to know how to make it happen. By the time we got in front of the Dr Pepper leadership team with our new cut, every single person – agency side and client side - was aligned around this track.

It's a rare thing to see a client work so hard to sell itself on an idea we wanted. I've never seen anything quite like it before. The agency was stunned. We're so used to being the ones pushing our clients to take a bit more "risk", but here they were pushing themselves while we sat on the sidelines. And sure enough, when all of the groundwork was in place, Dr Pepper indeed bought the song. (Ok, in truth, two versions of the commercial ran, one with the original track and a version with new track). In the end, the leadership at Dr Pepper was won over by the conviction of their own people, rather than the agency.

An outcome like the one I just shared – where better creative ideas are able to come to fruition – is not possible without a willingness and desire to treat every single client, no matter their pay grade, with respect. When you collaborate down and sideways – not just up the corporate ladder – it will pay off in the long run when you are able to assert your creative vision in a way that only a great, collaborative relationship allows you to.

Decide today to forge a strong, collaborative relationship with every client you have – whether they're above you, equal to you or below you – starting with the person that answers the phones at the front desk. I'm serious, make the effort and say "hi" to them too. I promise having a collaborative spirit with everyone will pay dividends.

And a final note on this: collaborating up, down and sideways isn't just about getting something. It's about treating people – all people – with respect, and that's just the right thing to do anyway.

17

COLLABORATION'S REWARDS

Above: The iconic ending of "There's a Soldier in All of Us", a commercial for Call of Duty: Black Ops - a project born of a very unlikely, but brilliant collaboration.

One of the best concepts I ever had the opportunity to work on was a commercial entitled "There's a Soldier in All of Us" for the Call of Duty franchise for Activision. In it, everyday people, in civilian clothes, are in the middle of a crazy firefight in some far-flung, war-torn location. The idea behind the commercial was simple: Anyone can play and anyone can be great on the Call of Duty virtual battlefield, because it's the ultimate level playing field. The commercial was conceived to be an invitation to everyone to join in the fun. It mixed everyday people with big-time celebrities, like Kobe Bryant and Jimmy Kimmel. Google it, or for you tablet readers, hit this link to watch:

https://www.youtube.com/watch?v=Pblj3JHF-Jo

I'm sharing this not to brag about my work (although I do hope you like the film). The story of how this commercial came to be is the real point. It was an unlikely collaboration of the first order.

In 2009, I was part of a pitch that helped bring the Call of Duty franchise to my ad agency at the time, TBWA/CHIAT/DAY. For the better part of a year, we struggled to execute a brilliant, but incredibly controversial idea – the very idea that won us the business; but ultimately, the client chose to spike that idea. Why risk controversy when you have a billion-dollar franchise that is guaranteed to succeed? You don't risk a billion-dollar franchise, turned out to be the answer.

Well, it's safe to say we were crushed. It felt like a wasted year and a waste of brilliant thinking.

Then, things seemed to go from bad to worse.

Activision decided to hire a new CEO. Who might that be? Eric Hirshberg, the Co-CEO/Chief Creative Officer of Deutsch LA, a rival agency to our agency, TBWA/CHIAT/DAY. (As an aside, Fortune 500 CEOs are rarely – if ever – plucked from Ad Agency creative departments, but Nike, feel free to call me.) And the Creative Director-turned-CEO's first order of business? Make the Call of Duty: Black Ops launch the biggest launch in gaming history. No small task.

Of course, the advertising campaign would be critical to achieving that goal.

So let's lay this out one more time just for kicks: my agency, TBWA/LA, would be pitching a new CEO ideas for Call of Duty: Black Ops. This new CEO was formerly the lead creative director at a rival ad agency. Oh boy, this should be fun.

To fully appreciate how uncomfortable the situation was, understand that Deutsch LA was truly a competitor agency, literally two streets down from TBWA/Chiat/Day/LA. Deutsch LA was growing tremendously and was competing for the same clients and was in the same pitches we were. There was a palpable sense of rivalry between us, especially since Deutsch had very recently taken away one of TBWA's most prestigious clients: Sony PlayStation. The new Activision CEO, Eric Hirshberg, was at the helm of that very effort in his former role as Co-CEO/Chief Creative Officer of Deutsch LA. There was no love lost at all between our agencies. In fact, we wondered if TBWA/Chiat/Day/LA was going to be fired on the spot. As it turned out, being so close to a critical launch, Activision opted to stick with TBWA/Chiat/Day/LA, for the moment, so we got a stay of execution, if you will.

So here comes our first meeting, where we must pitch a rival creative director-turned-CEO campaign ideas. He's now our boss for all intents and purposes. He's asking for ideas that help ensure that Call of Duty: Black Ops is the biggest entertainment launch in history. The situation – for both sides – was awkward, challenging and bizarre, to say the least.

However, from the beginning of this strange new relationship, I decided I was going to put my ego aside and collaborate, regardless of the outcome. It might be uncomfortable. It could well end badly. On the other hand, why not give it a shot?

Yes, I would collaborate. Frankly, I saw it as an opportunity.

After spinning my wheels with Activision for a year, getting nowhere, I chose to see Eric Hirshberg's arrival as a breath of fresh air. I now had a former Creative Director sitting on the other side of the table, who happened to now have the title, CEO. I surmised that since he was former advertising creative director, that at least meant he liked creative and could envision great creative – something many clients struggle to do. Oh, and as a CEO, he could write and cash checks to make that creative come to life. No, I wasn't about to let ego – mine or anyone else's – get in the way of opportunity.

Plus, there's that other pesky fact that he could fire us. So, yeah, park the ego.

Much to my surprise, in that first meeting in which we shared ideas with Eric, I discovered something interesting about this particular CEO – it's something you often see in successful creative thinkers: yes, you guessed it, he was a collaborator. (Maybe that's how he and current Deutsch North America, CEO, Mike Sheldon helped build the LA office from four or five people to one that has nearly 600 people working for it? Yeah, that would make sense, wouldn't it?)

The first thing Eric did was green light an advertising campaign, for another game, that had been collecting dust on someone's desk at Activision. He didn't even need to be formally pitched the idea – he just saw it and blessed it into production. That is an exceedingly rare thing for any client to do: approve an idea without a presentation. As in, it never happens. It was a clear indication of Eric's willingness to work with us in a collaborative way. I was also able to use this with my team as evidence that having a client with strong creative vision and taste, could be a very good thing for us, and not a threat. After all, we were already in production on a very cool idea, something we hadn't been able to accomplish for a year with this particular client, he put it into motion instantly.

Being a former Executive Creative Director, Eric also offered some opinions about who might direct the commercial for this newly green-lit idea. Well, this didn't seem to sit well with some people. This was somewhat understandable, since clients very rarely – if ever – offer up Director suggestions. Yet I remember feeling, at the time, that we were failing to appreciate the fact that Eric was – despite the strange circumstances – actually advocating for and pushing *our* ideas forward. And while it's true that it's not standard practice for a client to suggest directors to the agency, in this case, was it really that surprising given Eric's background as a creative leader? What was the big deal anyways? Why not listen to the suggestions? Why be threatened by these suggestions anyways, since they're just that: suggestions. I certainly wasn't threatened, but some people seemed to be. In my opinion, we were letting their egos get in the way. We, unfortunately, had the NP-attitude all the way.

After we pitched Eric ideas for Call of Duty: Black Ops, I walked him out, hoping to do a little damage control after the meeting – I worried that he picked up the non-collaborative vibe. I told him how excited I was he was the new CEO (okay, okay, it was a semi-true sentiment). How he should know – despite this strange relationship – that there would be no attitude from me or my team (absolutely true). Far from it, there would be enthusiasm. There would be collaboration. He could count on it.

I'm not sure Eric Hirshberg would even remember that chat. All I know, in addition to going into production on the first project he green-lit sight unseen, two months later he green-lit another production. This time, we were shooting an ambitious commercial for Call of Duty: Black Ops, the biggest video game franchise of all time. A commercial that would go on to get millions of views online and be celebrated by fans around the world – a film that I consider one of the best of my career. And so, I learned yet another lesson:

Good Collaboration Begets More Collaboration

But this unlikely collaboration would be tested mightily again as we entered the production phase.

Nowhere is there more pressure – outside of a pitch for a new client – than on the set of a multi-million dollar commercial. The whole concept's success is quite literally on the line. Money is burning up by the second. Sets, locations, celebrities and big-time directors are brought together to make magic in front of a camera for a limited time, and if you don't get the film right, you'll be "fixing it in post", which is what we say in the advertising industry when we don't capture what we needed on film on the day of the shoot. ("Post" refers to the post-production process where we add effects, add sound, adjust color and do a myriad of other changes and embellishments to the film. And there's only so much "fixing" of film you can do in post.)

It's in the middle of this insanity that I discover the CEO of Activision will be visiting the set to check on his multi-million-dollar production. He would be arriving in a helicopter with one of the stars of the commercial, Kobe Bryant of the Los Angeles Lakers.

Let's restate the situation: here you have a CEO, who was formerly the Chief Creative Officer of a rival agency, coming to the set of a commercial that I, and my team, came up with. As the agency creative director, I'm the one ultimately charged with controlling all aspects of the creative on the set.

Can you see how wrong this could go? I could have been threatened. I could have been defensive. I could have made the situation intolerable. Instead, I took the view that Eric Hirshberg would have opinions – strong ones, in fact – maybe even wrong ones. The commercial set, after all, was an environment he was used to being in control of too. This was going to be uncomfortable. This was going to be challenging.

This situation would make excellent collaboration nearly impossible, right?

As it turned out, no.

Indeed, that day on the set, Eric had some strong opinions. Some of them, I judged to be wrong at the time. And Eric, understanding the value of true collaboration himself, knew where to give and appreciated me standing my ground on certain ideas. But some of his ideas he pushed for had a strange effect on the commercial: they made it better – quite a bit better. What do you know? Strange how this collaboration stuff works. The commercial would not have happened without Eric Hirshberg. But more than that, in truth, it wouldn't have been nearly as good without Eric.

Oh, and, the epitaph on it all, in case you're wondering: Call of Duty: Black Ops went on to be the biggest selling entertainment launch ever – bigger than any Hollywood movie or any other video game at that time. The commercial was viewed nearly 8 million times online and was debated on CNN and Fox News (partly due to its somewhat controversial content).

Mission accomplished.

Collaboration – though always immensely challenging – has its rewards indeed.

18

COLLABORATE TO LEAD

Few of us will be leaders of many, but ALL of us must collaborate. Which is why this book doesn't focus on leadership, a subject matter that has been written about endlessly.

That said, a book on collaboration would not be complete without a quick look at its relationship to good – and bad – leadership.

So let's get to the point, because it's plain to see: the best leaders are excellent at collaborating with those who work with them and for them.

Don't believe me? Think about your favorite boss you've worked for. There were many traits you admired about this person, to be sure, but one of those – I'm willing to bet - was that he or she valued and respected your input. That favorite boss probably often put your ideas into action. In other words, they truly collaborated with you.

Now, conversely, think about the bosses you've liked the least. Among their unlikeable traits, at the top of the list – I'm willing to bet - was the sense that they did not seem to appreciate your role or your input. They rarely put your thinking into action. They rarely were interested in your ideas. Or perhaps, they even walked off with your ideas as if they were their own, failing to give you credit. In other words, they did not collaborate with you.

I am convinced the number one way to lose your best employees, as a leader, is to fail to collaborate well with them.

This lack of collaboration from people in leadership positions can manifest itself in many ways, such as: not allowing your employees to push back on your opinions, not dignifying their input, being unable to change your mind when evidence is presented by your employee that your perspective on a particular issue is indeed wrong, and the list goes on.

Speaking for myself, my lowest points of motivation throughout my own career have been when I feel unsupported, that my opinion counts little and my thinking is not appreciated by my superiors. When I feel my boss rules by fiat, cares little about my counsel or my ideas, I begin to withdraw. I begin, if I'm honest, to ponder if my skills would be better put to use somewhere else.

Wouldn't you agree that's true for you?

On the flipside, I've found that collaborative leaders are ones with lots of loyal followers. (And this is a good thing since leading is awfully hard if you don't have followers.) People love to work for and support superiors who demonstrate that they value and dignify their employee's ideas. Collaborative leaders know that it makes people feel appreciated and needed. Any job where people feel their boss appreciates them, is usually a much more rewarding and fulfilling one.

But good leaders don't just win loyal followers by being collaborative, they also consistently create better ideas. As we've established earlier in this book, ideas get better when they're exposed to other collaborative people. As a leader, those people that make your ideas better are most often ones that report to you. To do this effectively, every leader needs to surround themselves with experts who can help them make wise decisions and then collaborate with them - *brilliantly.*

Good leaders are eager to collaborate with their teams because they know other people make them and their ideas smarter.

American Presidents have cabinets for a reason. They can't possibly do everything, nor do they possess all the expertise on all the subjects they will be required to make critical decisions about. The President's cabinet is there to make him smarter, faster. To help him think beyond what he already knows and what he's already considered. To help him see the potential upside and downside to every single idea he considers, so he can make wiser, better decisions.

Your team is really no different than a President's cabinet – they are in essence a bunch of experts, with specific jobs, who report to you. By collaborating with them well, you and your decisions become wiser. Your ideas are made better.

For the leader who won't collaborate with his or her team, lack of motivation and ultimately attrition, are what awaits them. And while they may wake up today the leader of many, they will eventually wake up some distant tomorrow, the leader of few.

Ultimately, being a collaborative leader is not only better for your team, it's better for you.

But most importantly, it's better for your ideas.

Isn't that what it's all about?

19

LONG LIVE COLLABORATORS

Shortened careers.

Torpedoed projects.

Ideas that never come to fruition.

Immense talent that rots on the vine.

The list of what happens to those who won't collaborate is endless, unnecessary, and always unfortunate.

The fact is, as human beings, we were made to collaborate and our ideas depend on collaboration to survive and thrive. As we've seen, collaboration is not only inevitable, it's highly beneficial and, ultimately, essential in creating and bringing ideas to life.

For those that collaborate well, many of their best ideas will live and their careers will prosper. People seek out people that collaborate well – their iPhone is always ringing. Those that can't – or won't – collaborate, on the other hand, will suffer the unfortunate consequences.

Early in my advertising career I watched better creative thinkers go into obscurity, scraping out a living and a subpar career when they were capable of much more. Later, I watched Creative Directors with talent to burn denied positions that could have expanded their ability to make brilliant ideas – all because of their inability to collaborate.

I have seen peers alienate everyone around them only to find the industry doors suddenly closed. And we've all seen immensely talented people in professional sports burn-out franchise after franchise, with their refusal to be a team player, only to find themselves in early retirement, leaving their rare talents to rot and the pundits to ask "what if?".

We have noted, early on in this book, that perhaps the greatest CEO and marketer in history, Steve Jobs, got voted off the board of the company HE started because he alienated people. Those lost years for Steve Jobs were all part of his journey, to be sure, but we'll never know what might have happened had he stayed on to guide his company during that time.

I titled this book, Collaborate or Die, because the death of your ideas – and, at some premature point, your career as a creative person – is what will result if you cannot, or will not, collaborate.

In the end, collaboration – and the willingness to do it – is an issue of the heart. Can you find a way to see how other people can make you and your ideas, better? Can you control your ego? Can you trust the process? Can you understand it's about the idea, not about you? These actions are counter-intuitive to our human nature and not instinctual to me or anyone else, but they are essential to be a great collaborator.

Indeed, to be a great collaborator, you will have to fight your own human nature – your innate desire to put you and your ideas first. You will need empathy, to be able to see things from others' points of view. You will have to subjugate your big, fat ego. You will need to be a trustworthy person. You will need to be able to trust the process along the way. And finally, you will need to seek out and surround yourself with other people who do all of the above.

Otherwise, yes, you will find yourself out of the job you love, sculpting things people will never see, in your garage.

Long live Collaborators.

AFTERWORD

As is often the case in life, just when you're dispensing your wisdom about something – in this case, that something being collaboration – you find life challenges you on the very subject matter you're so sure you've mastered.

All during the writing of this book, situations arose in my workplace that would challenge my commitment to collaboration, forcing me to really think hard about what I was writing within these pages. Indeed, many of the chapters of this book were written as these various situations arose, adding new fodder and dimensions to the subject in real time. The collaborative hurdles I faced during this time often forced me to look in the mirror and realize I was at fault in certain situations where collaboration with other people had broken down. Other times, I saw behavior that only reinforced how deep the problem of creative people not being able to collaborate well because of ego, narcissism and pride really is.

Which lead me to add this final thought, with this book in the rear view mirror, about the subject of collaboration: you don't ever arrive at being a great collaborator, you have to work at being a great one every single day.

Some days, you will be great at collaborating with others, shaping and helping create brilliant ideas. Other days, you will fail when your big, fat ego asserts itself and destroys any chance of collaboration.

The fact is, becoming a great collaborator never stops being challenging, because every day the challenge, itself, changes – the people you're working with changes, the idea you're working on changes, even your role from project to project can change. Point is, your work environment, in which you're attempting to collaborate well with others, is all constantly in a state of flux. Which means, every day, for the rest of your career, your collaboration skills will be challenged anew.

So, in the end, I learned yet another thing about collaboration in the pursuit of great ideas: it's a marathon, not a sprint.

Here's to endurance, fellow collaborators.

ACKNOWLEDGMENTS

I want to thank the following people for their direct collaboration in the creation of this book: editor, Zoe Markham, University of Idaho Professor of Advertising, Mark Secrist, and designer, Adam Hale, for the cover.

I also want to thank some other fellow collaborators who were cited within this book: the remarkable marketing team at Taco Bell, you are the best clients an agency could hope for. My friends at Dr Pepper, I am so proud of the work we've done together. Eric Hirshberg for the improbable partnership and incredible opportunity you gave us on Call of Duty. Lee Clow, for teaching me by example.

Finally, thanks to the people who have demonstrated what great collaboration looks like throughout my career: Tom Moyer, Rob Schwartz, Jerry Gentile, Pete Favat, Vic Palumbo and Mike Sheldon.